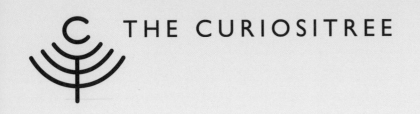

THE CURIOSITREE

A Chapter Two book
created by Amanda Wood and Mike Jolley

Brimming with creative inspiration, how-to projects, and useful information to enrich your everyday life, Quarto Knows is a favorite destination for those pursuing their interests and passions. Visit our site and dig deeper with our books into your area of interest: Quarto Creates, Quarto Cooks, Quarto Homes, Quarto Lives, Quarto Drives, Quarto Explores, Quarto Gifts, or Quarto Kids.

Curiositree: Human World © 2018 Quarto Publishing plc. Text © 2018 Amanda Wood. Illustrations © 2018 Andres Lozano. Concept, design and art direction by Mike Jolley.

First published in 2018 by Wide Eyed Editions, an imprint of The Quarto Group.
400 First Avenue North, Suite 400, Minneapolis, MN 55401, USA.
T (612) 344-8100 F (612) 344-8692 **www.QuartoKnows.com**

The right of Amanda Wood to be identified as the author and Andrés Lozano to be identified as the illustrator of this work has been asserted by them in accordance with the Copyright, Designs and Patents Act, 1988 (United Kingdom).

A catalog record for this book is available from the British Library.

ISBN 978-1-84780-992-6

The illustrations were created digitally
Set in Gill Sans

Published by Jenny Broom and Rachel Williams
Edited by Katie Cotton
Production by Jenny Cundill and Kate O'Riordan
Consultants: Professor Mark Pagel, FRS, and Jennie Roman

Manufactured in Dongguan, China TL052018

9 8 7 6 5 4 3 2 1

MIX
Paper from
responsible sources
FSC® C104723

A Visual C O M P E N D I U M *of Wonders from Human History*

HUMAN WORLD

By Amanda Wood & Mike Jolley · Illustrated by Andrés Lozano

WIDE EYED EDITIONS

Editor's Note

IF YOU LOOK UP "CURIOSITY" IN A DICTIONARY, IT WILL SAY SOMETHING LIKE, "A DESIRE TO KNOW OR TO LEARN." This sounds simple enough, but it is in fact one of the fundamental building blocks of our history. Along with our intelligence, curiosity has taken us from our early beginnings as hunter-gatherers to where we are today.

After all, without a desire to explore and explain, how would our ancestors, many thousands of years ago, have learned to control fire? How would we have first decided to try to tame and keep animals for food, rather than simply hunting them? How would we have had the courage to venture across the icy wilderness of the north to reach America from Asia? All of the great leaps forward in human history, from farming to the Renaissance and the Industrial Revolution, have been driven by our unquenchable desire to learn and to discover.

From our earliest origins to the year 1600, we have amassed a huge wealth of knowledge.

And these new discoveries and inventions are all interconnected, as this book will show you. For example, farming gave us more time, which led to huge developments in crafts, such as pottery. Better boat building allowed us to trade with other countries, meaning that we shared parts of our culture and language. We have learned to treat illness, sail the seas, speak and write in myriad languages, and create astonishing objects that do everything from telling the time to—more recently—telling us anything we want to know.

But, of course, we are still learning. As humans become more and more knowledgeable about our past, our future becomes ever harder to predict. The past few decades have seen men go to the moon, and the birth of the internet. Who knows what exciting developments and inventions are in store in the coming years? Set out on your own adventure in this book, and imagine how curiosity could change our world as never before.

Contents

Example 1

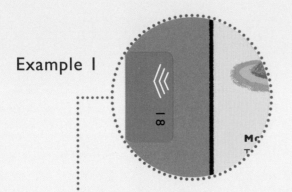

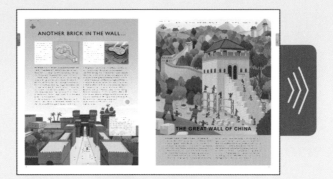

Follow the arrows and chart numbers...

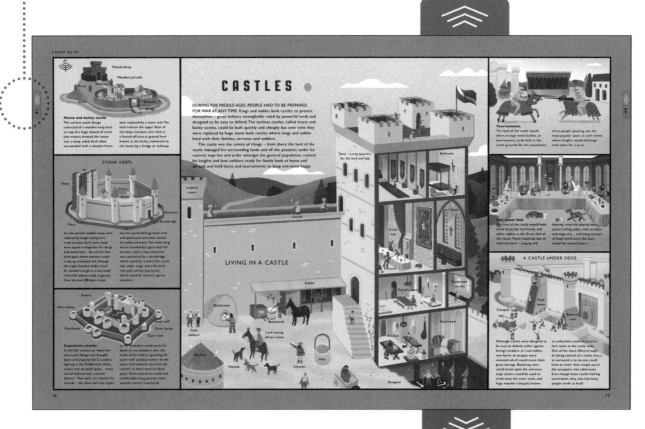

Example 2

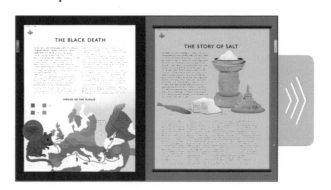

A note on dates:

Because there is no agreement on when time began, historians have agreed on a "Year One." For Christians, it is the birth of Jesus Christ, for Muslims the year of Mohammed's return to Mecca. **BCE** means "Before the Common Era"—that is, before Year One. This means that dates are counted backward, for example 100 BCE means 100 years before Year One.
CE means "Common Era." 100 CE means 100 years after Year One.
c. means circa, meaning "approximately."

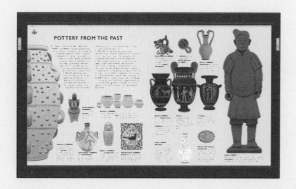

How to use this book

EVERY TIME YOU OPEN THIS BOOK, you can go on a different journey of discovery to find out more about the history of the human world. All of the charts in this book are color-coded according to the subject matter:

 Orange charts tell you about topics from **human history**, from the early evolution of humans to life in a medieval town.

 Yellow charts focus on developments in **art and culture**, from the evolution of writing to the great artists of the Renaissance.

 Blue charts look at **science, trade, and technology**, from early inventions to the world's oldest trading routes.

If you like, you can simply start the book at the beginning and continue reading until you get to the end. Use the colored ribbons like bookmarks, to mark your place or so that you can return to pages that you found especially interesting.

Alternatively, open the book wherever you like (you could even start right at the back) and then look for the colored arrows that you'll find in the left and right margins of each double-page spread. They'll take you backward or forward to other charts in the book containing information that is connected in some way to what you have just read.

Be curious, follow the arrows, and find out something new on every journey you take.

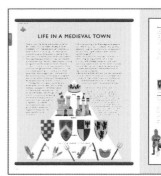

HUMAN BEGINNINGS

THE STORY OF HUMANS BEGINS AROUND 7 MILLION YEARS AGO, WHEN OUR EARLIEST APELIKE ANCESTORS FIRST APPEARED ON EARTH. Over the millions of years that followed, these early species diverged into many different kinds. Some lived alongside each other, competing for survival. By around 2–3 million years ago, the earliest species we might call "human" existed, although they were very different from us. Then, around 200,000 years ago, one particular kind of human appeared, *Homo sapiens*—which means the "wise man." By 40,000 years ago, they were the only type of human left.

Although they lived so very long ago, those early *Homo sapiens* were biologically the same as we are today. They had the same ability to use language—to talk and laugh and sing—the same long limbs that enabled them to run and climb and dance, and the same dextrous hands that allowed them to paint or make tools or fashion jewelry. They spread from their origins in Africa to eventually colonize the entire planet.

Early human and archaeological remains offer us important clues about our ancient past. The size and shape of fossilized bones, and the markings left by muscles, tell us how our predecessors looked and moved around, and how the size of their brains changed over time. Tools and other objects help us understand how early humans lived and how this evolved, as they moved from living in small groups of hunter-gatherers to the first farming communities—the beginning of civilization as we understand it today.

But this story of our early evolution is not necessarily complete. At any time, the discovery of a new fossil or other prehistoric remains can lead to a better understanding of how we lived and changed over time. The history of our human world may yet have surprises in store...

A LOOK AT HUMAN EVOLUTION

OUR EARLIEST ANCESTORS WERE HUMANLIKE ANIMALS KNOWN AS HOMININS. They evolved from early apes, and over millions of years developed important human characteristics—the ability to walk on two legs, a large and increasingly complex brain, the skill to make and use tools, and the ability to master their environment rather than being at its mercy. But this evolutionary journey involved not just one species, but many, with different types of hominin rising up and dying out along the way.

Our understanding of this evolutionary journey is full of gaps that new fossil finds might change at any time. What is clear is that it took millions of years for *Homo sapiens*—the first modern humans—

to appear, but only a few thousand years for us to advance beyond all other hominin species and colonize the entire planet.

• Humans are primates. Physical and genetic similarities show that modern humans and the great apes of Africa—chimpanzees, bonobos, and gorillas—are descended from a common ancestor that lived in Africa between 8 and 6 million years ago.

• Around 3 million years ago, the first hominins belonging to the genus *Homo* (the group that includes modern humans) appeared in Africa. A number of distinct groups of these early humans lived during this time but only our ancestor *Homo sapiens* survived.

• Most scientists currently recognize some 20 different species of early humans, although they don't all agree about how these species are identified and related. Scientists also debate what factors influenced the evolution and extinction of each species.

A. Ardipithecus group
- There were a number of species of these early "proto-humans."
- They are one of our earliest ancestors and took the first steps toward walking upright.
- Most were the size and shape of chimpanzees and were forest-dwelling.

B. Australopithecus
– Height 3.6 ft; weight 88 lb
- The first known hominins (humanlike creatures).
- Stood upright and walked on two feet but still climbed trees regularly.
- Had an apelike appearance, with projecting jaws and a small brain.
- Had long, powerful arms and long, curved fingers and toes for grasping branches.
- Used simple tools—stones for cracking open shells or sticks for breaking open termite nests.
- Mainly ate plants and insects and were the first of our ancestors to move out of the forests to live on the savanna.

C. Paranthropus group
- This group of early humans lived in woods and on grasslands, eating a variety of foods including grubs and plants.
- They had large teeth and powerful jaws that enabled them to chew on tough roots and other vegetation.

D. Homo habilis
– Height 5.2 ft; weight 110 lb
- With its bigger brain, this species is often thought of as the first human.
- Though its face protruded less than earlier hominins, it still retained many apelike features.
- Made simple tools from stone, flint, and wood.
- Ate meat, using stone tools to cut flesh from dead animals.
- This new diet provided more energy and may have led to a bigger brain.

E. Homo erectus
– Height 5.9 ft; weight 150 lb
- Had a bigger brain than Homo habilis and body proportions more similar to modern humans.
- Walked completely upright and could probably have run for long distances.
- Was likely the first of our ancestors to make hand axes.
- May have been able to use fire.
- Spread out from Africa to China and Europe.

F. Homo heidelbergensis
– Height 5.6 ft; weight 137 lb
- Had a large brow ridge, a larger braincase, and flatter face than previous early human species.
- The first early human species to live in colder climates; their short, wide bodies were probably an adaptation to conserving heat.
- Lived when evidence tells us that humans had learned to control fire.
- Likely used wooden spears, and was the first early human species to routinely hunt large animals.
- Also the first species to build shelters, creating simple dwellings out of wood and rock.

G. Homo floresiensis
– Height 3.5 ft; weight 66 lb
- One of the last surviving human species apart from Homo sapiens; became extinct some time within the last 50,000 years.
- Found on the island of Flores, in Indonesia.
- Had a tiny brain but, despite this, made stone tools, hunted for food, and may have used fire.
- Their small size may have resulted from island dwarfism—an evolutionary process that results from long-term isolation in a place with limited food resources and a lack of predators. Pygmy elephants also found on Flores, now extinct, showed the same adaptation.

H. Homo neanderthalensis
– Height 5.4 ft; weight 176 lb
- An early type of Homo sapiens that lived and became extinct during the last ice age, the Neanderthals were named after the Neander Valley, in Germany, where their bones were first found.
- Had strong muscular bodies and a prominent ridge of bone above eyes.
- Made clothing from animal skins for warmth.
- Made more sophisticated tools and used fire to help them chase and catch large animals such as mammoths.
- Lived and worked in family groups.

I. Homo sapiens
– Height 5.6 ft; weight 154 lb
- Very adaptable and with large brains.
- Developed spoken language and began to live in bigger groups, or tribes.
- Began to sew animal skins together to make clothes using bone needles and strips of leather as thread.
- Made advanced tools with handles—spears, harpoons, axes, and hammers.
- Made simple shelters from branches and animal hide.
- Created the first examples of art and the first musical instruments—bone flutes.

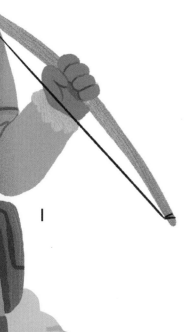

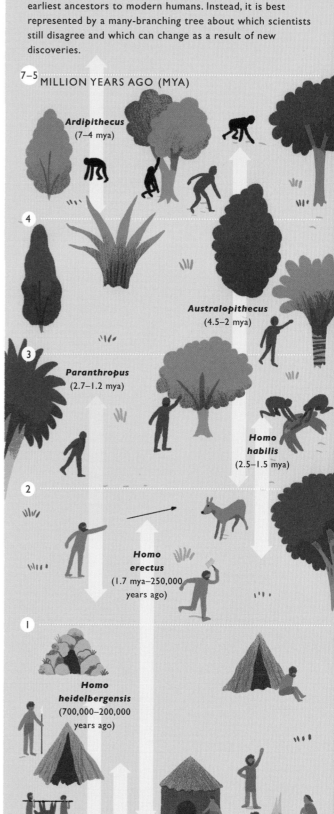

EVOLUTIONARY TREE

Contrary to popular belief, the evolution of humans is not a straight road that takes us in a neat sequence from our earliest ancestors to modern humans. Instead, it is best represented by a many-branching tree about which scientists still disagree and which can change as a result of new discoveries.

7–5 MILLION YEARS AGO (MYA)

Ardipithecus (7–4 mya)

4

Australopithecus (4.5–2 mya)

3

Paranthropus (2.7–1.2 mya)

Homo habilis (2.5–1.5 mya)

2

Homo erectus (1.7 mya–250,000 years ago)

1

Homo heidelbergensis (700,000–200,000 years ago)

Homo neanderthalensis (400,000–35,000 years ago)

Homo floresiensis (100,000–50,000 years ago)

Homo sapiens (200,000 years ago to present)

TODAY

THE EVOLUTIONARY ROAD

FOUND ALMOST EVERYWHERE ACROSS THE FACE OF THE EARTH, early hominin fossils and other archaeological remains like tools and footprints offer us clues about our prehistoric past. These remains not only tell us how our physical appearance changed over time, but also about how we lived in our environment and the many milestones we passed on the long road to civilization.

1–7 MILLION YEARS AGO

7 million years ago (mya):
The first hominins appear, descended from early primates.

Between 4.1 and 1.9 mya:
Remains show us that hominins gradually adapt to regular bipedal (two-legged) walking.

By 2.6 mya:
Early hominins start to use basic tools made of stone and wood, starting the Stone Age. They eat more meat, cutting flesh from dead animals. The extra energy obtained may have led to the evolution of a larger brain.

By 1.6 mya:
First major technological innovation takes place with the making of hand axes. This technology persists for more than 1.2 million years.

100,000–1 MILLION YEARS AGO

250,000 years ago:
Early humans begin to communicate with symbols, with evidence of "crayons" (sticks and chunks of pigment). The use of fire for cooking food probably becomes widespread.

280,000 years ago:
First stone blades and grinding stones appear.

By 400,000 years ago:
Early humans make purpose-built shelters—wooden huts—and invent wooden thrusting spears to help them hunt large animals.

By 700,000 years ago:
Remains indicate that early humans had probably learned how to light fires.

By 800,000 years ago:
Early pre-modern humans learn to control fire and create hearths. This is also the beginning of the most rapid increase in early human brain size.

200,000 years ago:
Modern humans (*Homo sapiens*) evolve in Africa. End of the rapid increase in brain size.

Between 135,000 and 100,000 years ago:
Modern humans make necklaces of animal teeth, claws, and beads of shell, the oldest known jewelry. Use is made of animal skins for clothing. Complex speech develops.

By 130,000 years ago:
Modern humans begin to trade—exchanging goods and resources, like tin, over long distances.

By 104,000 years ago:
Modern humans become capable of capturing fast and dangerous prey with an increasing array of tools such as atlatls (spear throwers).

By 100,000 years ago:
Earliest recorded purposeful burial, although there is some evidence that early hominins, c.500,000 years ago, also buried their dead.

Between 100,000 and 32,000 years ago:
Neanderthals create rare carved plaques and pendants.

3,500–100,000 YEARS AGO

By 20,000 years ago:
First evidence of clay vessels.

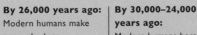

By 26,000 years ago:
Modern humans make woven baskets.

By 30,000–24,000 years ago:
Modern humans became capable of making well-fitted clothing using bone needles.

By 35,000 years ago:
Modern humans create the first musical instruments, including bone flutes, drums, and various types of percussion instruments.

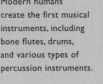

By 40,000–35,000 years ago:
Oldest cave art. Later, Stone Age artisans create the spectacular murals at Lascaux and Chauvet in France.

50,000 years ago:
The "great leap forward." People begin burying their dead ritually; create clothes from animal hides; and develop more complex hunting techniques, like pit traps, and tools such as the hafted ax and the bow and arrow.

By 90,000 years ago:
Modern humans make specialized tools for fishing.

12,000 years ago:
The beginning of the Neolithic Age, when humans become a turning point in the history of life on Earth, by controlling the growth and breeding of certain plants and animals. Herding and farming follow.

By 10,500 years ago:
Food production leads to settlements (villages, towns, cities) and the human population grows.

5,300 years ago:
Stone Age ends and Bronze Age begins. Humans begin to smelt and work copper and tin, and use them in place of stone tools.

5,200 years ago:
Earliest known writing.

By 4,000 years ago:
Pottery is used to make an increasingly complex array of objects.

By 3,500 years ago
The Sumerians of Mesopotamia develop the world's first civilization.

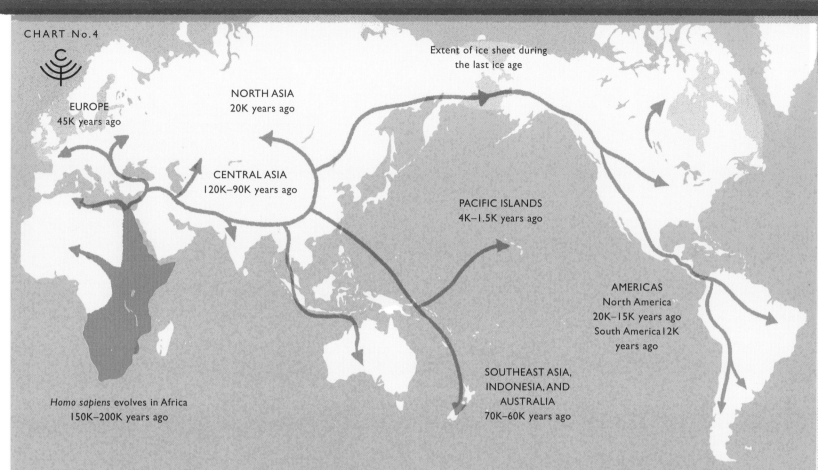

Extent of ice sheet during the last ice age

EUROPE
45K years ago

NORTH ASIA
20K years ago

CENTRAL ASIA
120K–90K years ago

PACIFIC ISLANDS
4K–1.5K years ago

AMERICAS
North America
20K–15K years ago
South America 12K
years ago

SOUTHEAST ASIA,
INDONESIA, AND
AUSTRALIA
70K–60K years ago

Homo sapiens evolves in Africa
150K–200K years ago

HOMO SAPIENS RULE THE WORLD

DURING A TIME OF DRAMATIC CLIMATE CHANGE 200,000 YEARS AGO, OUR SPECIES—*HOMO SAPIENS*, THE MODERN HUMAN—EVOLVED IN AFRICA. From a tiny population we spread, directed in our wanderings by climate, environment, and competition—both with other early hominins, and with the large predators for whom we were prey. We spread out of Africa, then throughout the Europe and Asia land mass. With the help of the ice sheets and shallower seas of the last ice age, we crossed continents—into Australasia, and finally the New World of the Americas. With the invention of boats we conquered the seas, settling on even the remotest Pacific islands.

No one knows for sure what drove us—a search for food or simply a more hospitable place to live, a change in the climate, or simply our nomadic spirit—but in time the human footprint could be found in almost every place on Earth.

PEOPLE OF THE WORLD

Over thousands of years, as we spread across the planet, differences began to emerge between some populations of *Homo sapiens*. Often these differences were linked to environment. Skin color, for example, was influenced by the intensity of sunlight in different climates so those living in cooler regions evolved to have less melanin (dark pigment) as they needed less protection against the damaging effects of the sun's rays. But there were differences too in language and culture that emerged and evolved over thousands of years, in the shelters people built and the clothes that they wore, the food they ate and the beliefs they held. As the climate shifted and sea levels rose and fell, so some populations became isolated, their differences becoming consolidated as they bred among themselves without any influence from outside. Where contact was reestablished, the characteristics of individual populations became blended over time to give us the great and wonderful variation of humankind that we can see in our world today.

SURVIVING THE ICE AGE

ICE AGES OCCUR WHEN THE TEMPERATURE OF OUR PLANET DROPS, PERHAPS BY JUST A FEW DEGREES, BUT ENOUGH FOR ICE TO BUILD UP IN GREAT SHEETS, COVERING STRETCHES OF LAND AND SEA. There have been many ice ages in Earth's history, most taking place long before humans appeared, but the last one occurred over 100,000 years ago and lasted until about 18,000 years ago. At its height, much of Europe and North America was frozen solid. The oceans froze and sea levels fell by over 328 feet (100 meters), turning many parts of the seabed into dry land.

By the time the ice retreated, there was only one species of hominin left alive—*Homo sapiens*. And thanks to the shallower seas and the bridges formed by the great ice sheets, we had spread even farther across the planet from our origins in Africa, migrating from Asia to the Americas.

From the moment the ice sheets retreated, releasing back huge swathes of land that had been previously uninhabitable, modern humans went through a period of rapid development, turning to farming and thereby setting the stage for the rise of modern civilization.

NEANDERTHAL HUNTERS

The Neanderthals were an early type of human that appeared in Europe about 400,000 years ago and died out during the last ice age. Though they were similar to *Homo sapiens*, they are usually considered to be a different species.
• Their bodies were adapted to survive in colder environments—with huge noses to warm the cold, dry air that they had to breathe, and short, stocky bodies to preserve warmth and energy. They also had strong jaws and teeth to help them tear meat from bone and to help in the cleaning of animal skins.
• They made tools for hunting, cutting food, and shaping wood.
• They sheltered in caves or made simple shelters from branches and the skins of animals.
• They wore simple clothes made from knotting and tying animal skins together.
• Since the cold meant there were fewer plants to eat, the Neanderthals ate a lot of meat, stripping the flesh from dead animals and hunting down deer, horses, and mammoths for food.
• They used fire, both to warm themselves and to help with hunting large prey such as mammoths and rhinos, chasing them over cliff edges with the help of burning branches.
• Some experts think that the Neanderthals used simple language. Being able to communicate would have been a big advantage when hunting and trying to avoid danger.

EARTH DURING THE LAST ICE AGE

About 20,000 years ago, the last ice age reached its height. Then over a third of the Earth's surface was overed in ice, the last remnants of which are the ice sheets that cover Antarctica and Greenland today.

During the last ice age, creatures such as mammoths, mastodons, and saber-toothed tigers still roamed the Earth alongside early humans.

Mastodon

Sabre-toothed tiger   Mammoth

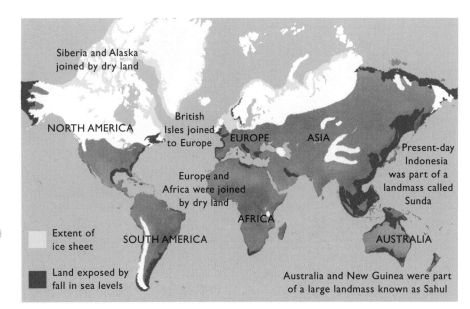

Siberia and Alaska joined by dry land

NORTH AMERICA

British Isles joined to Europe

EUROPE   ASIA

Present-day Indonesia was part of a landmass called Sunda

Europe and Africa were joined by dry land

AFRICA

SOUTH AMERICA

AUSTRALIA

Extent of ice sheet

Land exposed by fall in sea levels

Australia and New Guinea were part of a large landmass known as Sahul

MAMMOTH HUNTERS OF THE LAST ICE AGE

By the end of the last ice age, modern humans were the only hominins left alive. They had spread from their origins in Africa to colonize even the most inhospitable places on Earth. On the freezing plains of eastern Europe, one group of such humans had become experts at hunting large animals thanks to their increased intelligence and adaptability. Compared to the Neanderthals, these mammoth-hunter communities were more sophisticated and well developed.
• They made more complex tools than the Neanderthals, including spear throwers, known as atlatls, that allowed them to attack dangerous prey, such as mammoths, from a safe distance.
• They used mammoth bones and skins to make their homes, providing them with shelter from the snow and wind.
• They sewed mammoth skins together using bone needles to make warm, well-fitting leather clothes for the winter months, including hats, boots, and mittens.
• They could make their own fire by knocking stones together to make sparks for catching tinder alight.
• They made beads and bracelets from shells, bones, and tusks, and created some of the world's first musical instruments—drums made from mammoth skulls and simple flutes fashioned from hollow bones.

THE EVOLUTION OF MODERN HUMANS

ALL HUMAN BEINGS LIVING TODAY BELONG TO THE SPECIES *HOMO SAPIENS*. Like the other early humans that lived alongside us, we gathered and hunted food and evolved behaviors that helped us survive in a changing, challenging world. But over time, it became clear that human beings were unique. Our complex brains enabled us to interact with each other and with our surroundings in new and different ways and helped us to adapt quickly to changes in our environment. We made specialized tools, and used those tools to make other tools. We learned how to control fire and built shelters to live in.

We created social networks, sometimes over great distances, and exchanged resources over wide areas, living together in bigger and bigger groups. We created art, music, personal adornments, rituals, and a complex symbolic world. We spread to every continent and vastly expanded our numbers, altering the world around us and eventually outcompeting all other species of hominin until they disappeared altogether. Although we don't yet know everything about our evolution, with every new discovery we continue to learn more about who we are.

WALKING ON TWO LEGS

No one knows for sure why early hominins started walking on two legs. Perhaps it was the result of climate change—as the Earth cooled, the forests shrank and our ancestors had to travel farther to find food. With their upright posture, broader knee joints, double-curved (shock-absorbing) spine, not to mention stronger hip and longer thigh bones, early humans could walk farther and faster than primates (and had their hands free to carry things or throw spears).

By the time *Homo sapiens* appeared, the human skeleton had evolved even further. Apart from larger brains, modern humans also had lighter skeletons—possibly as a result of our ability to use technology to help us rather than relying on brute strength alone. Our skulls had become more rounded, with straight foreheads, less developed jaws, and smaller teeth, reflecting a diet of cooked food which is easier to chew and digest.

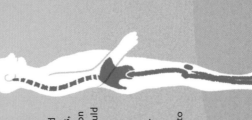

Chimpanzee spine

Human spine, showing the double-curve

Clothing

There is no easy way to tell when humans first started to wear clothing, but one clue has come from studying body lice. These insects first appeared around 170,000 years ago, and as they live on clothes, clothing must have existed then. Over time, *Homo sapiens* developed new technologies to help them make more suitable clothing, like sewing, using bone needles and, later, cloth from spun plant fibers.

BRAIN SIZE

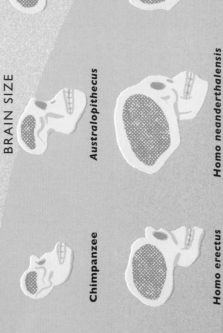

Chimpanzee

Australopithecus

Homo habilis

Homo erectus

Homo neanderthalensis

Homo sapiens

By 50,000 years ago, humans benefited from a highly developed brain, but having a big brain gave us a big problem. At the same time that our brains were growing larger, we were evolving to walk upright, with narrow hips and a narrower birth canal as a result. If we were born as physically mature as, say, an infant gorilla, our heads would be so big that it would be impossible for our parents

to give birth to us. The solution: human babies began to be born far less developed than other newborn primates, and far more helpless. We needed to be looked after by our parents for our first years. This gave us time to absorb the wisdom of our elders—the history of our tribe, tips on how to hunt, how to make fire, or tools, or any of the other skills that could help us survive.

Art and abstract thinking

One of the most striking differences between *Homo sapiens* and other early humans is their great ability for abstract thinking and creating art. They left behind them a dazzling variety of symbolic works including the earliest

with complex sound capabilities, and spectacular animal paintings that were often accompanied by numerous geometric symbols.

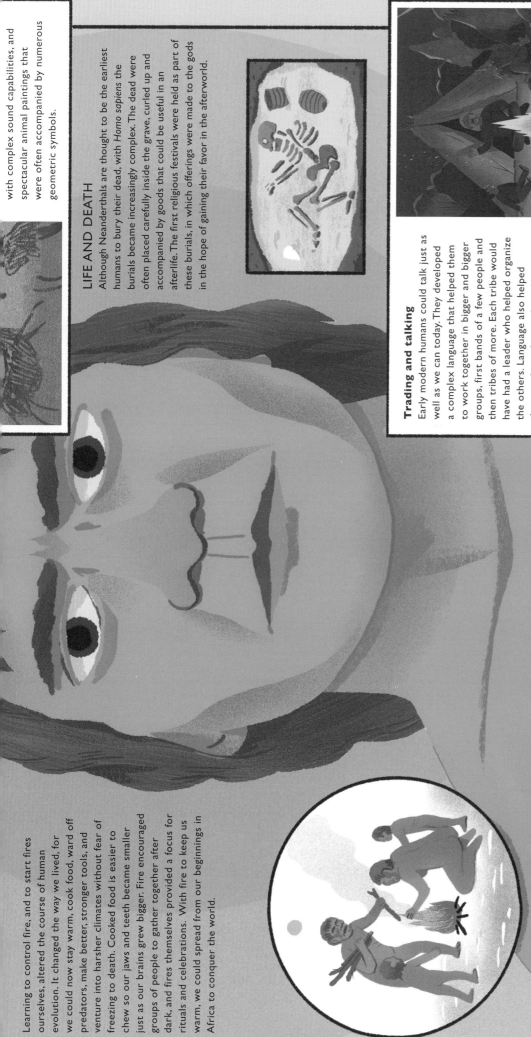

Learning to control fire, and to start fires ourselves, altered the course of human evolution. It changed the way we lived, for we could now stay warm, cook food, ward off predators, make better, stronger tools, and venture into harsher climates without fear of freezing to death. Cooked food is easier to chew so our jaws and teeth became smaller just as our brains grew bigger. Fire encouraged groups of people to gather together after dark, and fires themselves provided a focus for rituals and celebrations. With fire to keep us warm, we could spread from our beginnings in Africa to conquer the world.

LIFE AND DEATH

Although Neanderthals are thought to be the earliest humans to bury their dead, with *Homo sapiens* the burials became increasingly complex. The dead were often placed carefully inside the grave, curled up and accompanied by goods that could be useful in an afterlife. The first religious festivals were held as part of these burials, in which offerings were made to the gods in the hope of gaining their favor in the afterworld.

Trading and talking

Early modern humans could talk just as well as we can today. They developed a complex language that helped them to work together in bigger and bigger groups, first bands of a few people and then tribes of more. Each tribe would have had a leader who helped organize the others. Language also helped them trade tools or other objects with other tribes, and pass on useful information about their experiences.

TOOL MAKING

The ability to make tools is one of the key things that helped humans climb to the top of the food chain. By inventing tools, early humans were able to accomplish tasks that human bodies alone could not, such as using a spear to kill prey. As well as hunting, tools were useful for other activities,

from preparing food to starting fires or harvesting grain.

Hominins started to use stone tools regularly 2.5 million years ago, splitting pebbles to create sharp edges for cutting, chopping, and scraping. Then a million years or so later, early humans began to make hand axes,

shaping both sides of a piece of stone into a tool used for butchering and skinning prey, digging soil, and cutting wood or other plant materials.

With the arrival of modern humans, tool technology began to gather momentum. First came hafted tools, where a piece of bone, metal, or

stone was attached to a haft (a handle or strap). This made the artifact more useful by allowing it to be shot (in the case of an arrow), thrown (spear), or used with more effective leverage (ax or hammer). Hafted tools were the first example of humans putting two separate elements together to create

a single more efficient tool, paving the way toward the world of complex tool-making that would follow.

As well as stone tools, early humans also made a variety of other specialized tools, including fish hooks, bows and arrows, spear throwers, and sewing needles.

Split pebble

Hand ax

Hafted ax

Bone fish hook

Harpoon

Atlatl (spear-thrower)

Bow and arrow

10,000 – Farming begins in the Fertile Crescent

9000 – Earliest walled settlement built at Jericho and world's oldest temple, Göblekli Tepe, in Turkey

8000 – Small towns and communities develop with the spread of farming

7000 – Pottery develops; first use of bricks for building; sea levels rise separating Great Britain from Europe

6250 – Catal Huyuk, one of the first towns, is at its largest

5000 – Megalithic period begins in Europe with the building of huge stone temples and ceremonial sites; farming begins in the Nile Valley

BCE

LIFE IN THE ANCIENT WORLD

ONE OF THE FIRST TURNING POINTS IN THE DEVELOPMENT OF HUMANS WAS LEARNING TO WALK UPRIGHT. A SECOND MAJOR DEVELOPMENT WAS LANGUAGE, WHICH HUMANS HAD BY ABOUT 200,000 YEARS AGO. Then, about 190,000 years later, humans invented something that would change the world: farming. This marked the start of civilization, when we moved from being nomadic hunter-gatherers and started to live in small farming communities. These permanent settlements evolved over time into towns and eventually into magnificent cities, a pattern that started in the Middle East and was then repeated at different times in China, India, Europe, and later the Americas.

The ancient world, from around 10,000 BCE to the fall of the Roman Empire in 476 CE, was an age of great civilizations that rose and fell, when humans created incredible buildings, crafted amazing objects, and made huge strides forward in knowledge. Some of our greatest inventions come from these early times—the ability to make metal, create pottery, or weave cloth; the invention of writing or the wheel; the creation of the first laws; or the belief in gods to help explain aspects of the world that were then beyond our understanding.

4500 – World's first cities are established in Mesopotamia

4000 – Pacific settlers leave Southeast Asia and eventually colonize the islands of Polynesia

3500 – Farmers settle in India's Indus Valley; the wheel is invented

3200 – People in Mesopotamia and Egypt learn to make bronze

3100 – Early forms of writing are created in Sumer and Egypt

3000 – Work begins on the building of Stonehenge in Britain

2500 – Great Pyramid of Giza is completed in Egypt

2000 – Assyria becomes a kingdom

1900 – Iron Age starts in western Asia; Minoans build the first palaces on Crete

1792 – Hammurabi creates the kingdom of Babylon

1600 – Shang dynasty rules in China's Yellow River valley; Myceneans become rich and powerful

1450 – Myceneans from Greece take control of Crete; Egyptian Empire is at its largest

1200–900 – Olmecs and Chavin civilizations grow in Central and South America

1000 – Phoenicians become the most successful traders of the ancient world

900 – Assyrian Empire expands

800 – Celtic tribes appear in Europe

221 – Qin Shi Huang becomes first emperor of China

206 – Han dynasty starts in China

146 – Greece becomes part of the Roman Empire

321 – Mauryan Empire begins in India

300 – Mayans begin to build stone cities

400 – Persian Empire is at its height

539 – Babylon becomes part of the Persian Empire

509 – Rome becomes a republic

600 – The kingdom of Babylon is restored under Nebuchadnezzar II

700 – Ancient Greek civilization grows to be the most powerful in the Mediterranean

0 BCE

CE

30 – Egypt becomes part of the Roman Empire; Christian religion is established after the death of Jesus Christ

72 – Work begins on the Colosseum in Rome, Italy

100 – Paracas, Nazca, and Moche cultures flourish in northern Peru

117 – Roman Empire is at its height

278 – Celts spread into Asia

395 – Roman Empire splits into the Eastern and Western Empires

476 – Western Roman Empire falls

THE FIRST FARMERS

WE HUMANS HAVE COME A LONG WAY SINCE OUR ANCESTORS FIRST WALKED THE EARTH 2.5 MILLION YEARS AGO. For thousands of years, we lived as nomadic hunter-gatherers, moving from place to place in search of food and defending ourselves from wild animals. But toward the end of the Stone Age, around 12,000 years ago, in a period known as the Neolithic, a fundamental change took place that transformed the way that humans lived. Instead of just collecting wild grains and seeds for

food, they began to plant them, growing crops and keeping animals. They were the world's first farmers.

The emergence of farming, or agriculture, meant that people were able to produce their own reliable source of food and thereby live permanently in one place. This in turn heralded the appearance of the first settlements and, in time, to the creation of the world's earliest civilizations—in Mesopotamia, Egypt, India, and China.

A. **Early cattle** were domesticated from wild breeds such as the aurochs. Goats and sheep were some of the first animals to be domesticated for milk and meat. Later, larger animals such as oxen and horses were also kept for plowing and transportation.

B. **Walls** were built to form enclosures for animals and to protect crops, as well as to keep out wild animals or other humans.

C. **Dogs** were the first domesticated animals, possibly as far back as 30,000 BCE.

D. In addition to their use for food, the **skins** of domesticated animals provided a further resource for clothing.

E. **Permanent shelters** of wood, mud brick, and thatch were built.

F. Early settlements were often sited near **rivers** where the land was fertile and there was a plentiful supply of water.

G. In addition to **planting cereal crops** and keeping animals, humans still gathered fruit, seeds, and nuts from the surrounding area and hunted wild animals for their meat and skins.

H. The first **pottery** objects appeared around this time—bowls and pots allowed liquid to be boiled over a fire so soups and stews could be made.

I. Cereal grains such as wheat, millet, barley, rice, and maize were ground into flour using **stone tools.**

4750 BCE
Maize is grown in Central America.

4500 BCE
Farming spreads to Northern Europe

2100 BCE
Farming of maize spreads to North America.

***10,000 BCE**
Neolithic farming starts in Mesopotamia.

***4000 BCE**
Agriculture develops independently in Africa

***5500 BCE**
Farming begins in the Andes. Guinea pigs and llamas are kept for food and clothing.

NORTH AMERICA

SOUTH AMERICA

7000 BCE
Farming spreads to Southern Europe from the Middle East

2500 BCE
In Central Asia the Bactrian camel is domesticated

EUROPE

AFRICA

ASIA

6000 BCE
Agriculture becomes established in the Indus Valley

2500 BCE
The practice of farming spreads through Southeast Asia

***8000 BCE**
Rice growing begins independently in China.

AUSTRALIA

KEY TO MAP

Fertile Crescent

* Farming starts independently

Main crops

Barley

Millet

Wheat

Domesticated animals

Bactrian camel

Buffalo

Cattle

Chicken

Goat

Guinea pig

Pig

Turkey

Yak

Maize

Rice

Llama

Sheep

THE SPREAD OF AGRICULTURE

Farming started independently at different times and in different parts of the world, as you can see from this map. The very first evidence of farming is from around 10,000 BCE in ancient Mesopotamia, in an area of land that stretched from Egypt to the Persian Gulf. It was watered by several important rivers, including the Nile, Tigris, and the Euphrates, and the soil was so rich that it is often referred to as the Fertile Crescent. In addition to the main crops shown above, other food was grown—figs and legumes in Western Asia and Europe; potatoes, squash, and peanuts in the Americas; soybeans in China. And, in addition to food, other crops were also cultivated, such as cotton, flax and hemp for clothing, and medicines like cocoa and coffee.

41

23

THE FIRST TOWNS

TOWARD THE END OF THE STONE AGE, HUMANS HAD BEGUN TO SETTLE IN ONE PLACE. They planted crops instead of gathering food from the wild and learned how to make bricks from mud and clay to build permanent homes instead of living on the move.

Over time, small villages grew into the world's first towns, the earliest of which may date back 10,000 years. Living together, the people could work in a community to farm the land so they had a reliable source of food. Their buildings provided shelter not just for the people, but as a place to store tools and extra food in case of shortages. They could also exchange spare goods with other tribes, which would eventually lead to a trade in goods that crossed the world.

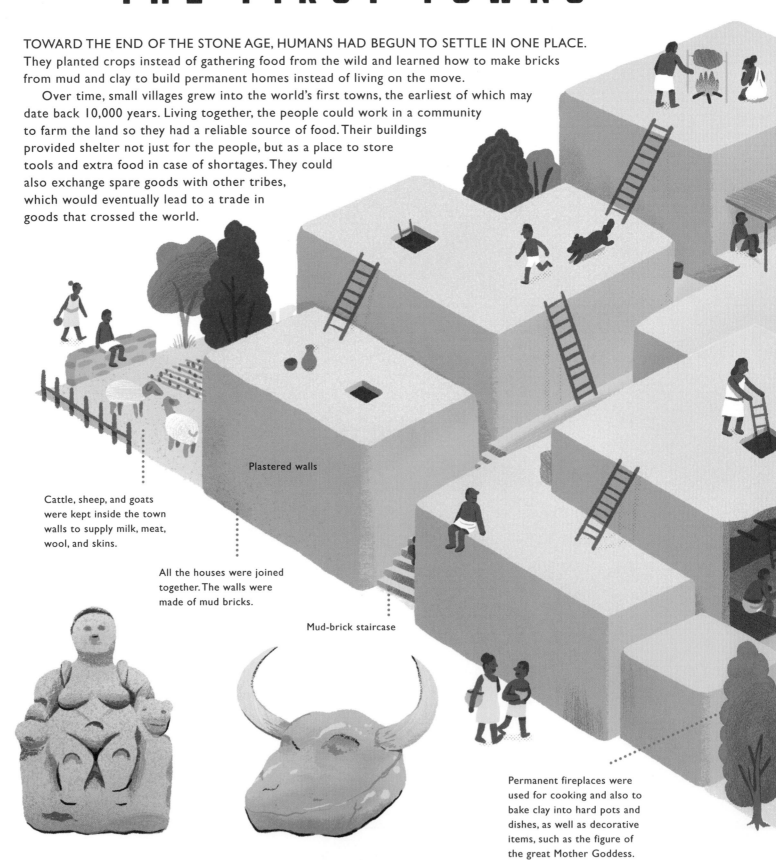

Plastered walls

Cattle, sheep, and goats were kept inside the town walls to supply milk, meat, wool, and skins.

All the houses were joined together. The walls were made of mud bricks.

Mud-brick staircase

Permanent fireplaces were used for cooking and also to bake clay into hard pots and dishes, as well as decorative items, such as the figure of the great Mother Goddess. shown on the left.

Mother Goddess clay figure from Catal Huyuk

Clay bull's head with real horns

Reed roof

The town roofs were where most daily activities took place—weaving, curing animal skins, cooking, and eating.

Staying in one place had disadvantages too. The settlements were vulnerable to raiders who came to steal food and livestock, so, for protection, walls were built around towns and houses were packed tightly together so any attackers would find it hard to gain access.

Early settlements so far discovered include Gobekli Tepe in modern Turkey and Jericho in modern Palestine. One of the largest early towns yet discovered, Catal Huyuk, also in Turkey, was home to over 7,000 people over 6,000 years ago. It was formed of many mud-brick houses, clustered together like a honeycomb. For security, there were no pathways between the dwellings. Instead, people moved around using the roofs and accessed their homes through a hole in the ceiling.

Some houses had interior walls painted with scenes of everyday life or geometric patterns.

Wooden beams

When someone died, the body was left outside to rot before being buried at a later date beneath the floor of the house.

The town roofs were accessed by ladders. If the town was attacked, the ladders would be pulled up.

As well as living spaces, there were shrine rooms where people prayed to their gods and offerings could be made.

Each house had one main room and another smaller one for storage. There was a hearth below the roof hole for cooking, and a raised earth platform for sleeping.

Clay pot

Woven blanket

POTTERY FROM THE PAST

POTTERY IS ONE OF THE MOST ANCIENT CRAFTS ON EARTH. It has existed ever since early humans discovered that clay could be dug up, mixed with water, molded into a shape, and baked hard in a fire. Clay deposits can be found in many countries, so shards of pots many thousands of years old have been found at archaeological sites all over the world. And because it is hard-wearing, lots of pottery remains have survived to tell us their own story of human evolution.

• Even though the earliest pottery dates back over 30,000 years, the craft did not truly develop until 20,000 years later, when, with the advent of farming, people began to live in permanent settlements and needed more sophisticated vessels in which to keep, cook, and carry their produce.

• Methods of firing pottery at high enough temperatures to turn it from raw clay into fine ceramic did not develop until around 1,500 years ago with the invention of kilns and furnaces.

• As societies became more complex, individuals began to specialize in different jobs and those responsible for making pottery were able to hone their skills. The quality and variety of their products increased, and soon they were providing goods not just for their community but for trade with other cultures.

• The potter's wheel, invented in Mesopotamia around 6000 BCE, revolutionized pottery production. Shaping (or "throwing") pots on a flat, spinning wheel was much quicker than making them out of slabs or coils. Pots were some of the first objects to be mass-produced by humans.

Czech Republic, 29,000 BCE
The oldest known **ceramic** object is this so-called Venus figurine.

Bowl   Beaker   Food vessel

Britain, c.1200 BCE
Early pots were shaped by hand or built up from slabs or coiled lengths of rolled **clay**. The decoration was formed by pressing patterns into the soft clay before it was fired.

Knossos, 1700 BCE
Hundreds of these huge earthenware storage jars called **pithoi** were found in the Minoan palace of Knossos. They would have been used for storing grain and liquids and many were as tall as an adult.

Catal Huyuk, 7000 BCE
This **earthenware** pot found in Turkey has geometric designs hand-painted onto the surface.

Egypt, c.2500 BCE
These **canopic jars** stored the different internal organs of a person to be mummified. The lids bore the heads of different gods.

Mesopotamia, 9000 BCE
Glazes were first developed for use on ceramic tiles. They gave the clay a glassy skin when heated and made it waterproof.

South America, 500 BCE
Many of the artifacts of the Chavin people were in the shape of animals, such as this **jaguar stirrup pot**.

This **pottery** spoon was made by the Pueblo Indians of **North America c.1100 CE**.

China, 1500 BCE
Stoneware was created in China this early thanks to the invention of kilns that could fire pots at higher temperatures.

Greece, 700–400 BCE
Ancient **Greek vases** are famous for their silhouetted depictions of Greek culture.

Amphora were used for carrying wine. This one shows the legendary warrior Heracles capturing the three-headed dog Cerberus.

Krater were used for mixing wine and water at drinking parties. This example shows the mythical chariot race that gave rise to the Olympic Games.

A **hydria** was a pitcher designed to carry water. This one portrays women gathering to fill their hydriai at a fountain.

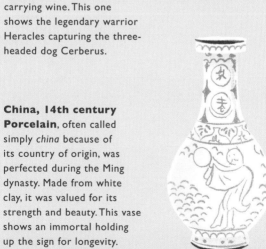

China, 14th century
Porcelain, often called simply *china* because of its country of origin, was perfected during the Ming dynasty. Made from white clay, it was valued for its strength and beauty. This vase shows an immortal holding up the sign for longevity.

Persia, 12th century
Lusterware is a type of pottery or porcelain with a metallic glaze that gives the effect of iridescence. It was popular in painted pottery from Persia, such as this plate showing a soldier slaying a leopard.

China, 210 BCE
Pottery is often found in burial sites. This warrior made of **terra-cotta** (a type of earthenware) was one of 7,000 life-size figures found in the tomb of China's first emperor.

MAKING A MARK—THE FIRST ARTISTS

HUMANS HAVE BEEN MAKING WORKS OF ART FOR MORE THAN 75,000 YEARS, from pottery figures to jewelry and decorative patterns carved into bone or painted on walls. Over time and across cultures, the style of visual art has changed, showing different traditions and beliefs as well as the range of materials available to those early artists as they tried new ways of reflecting the world around them.

• The earliest surviving artworks that depict animals and occasionally people were made around 40,000 years ago, painted onto the walls of caves during the height of the Ice Age.

• Some early works of art seem to have a religious or magical purpose, possibly representing the gods in which people believed or made to convey a blessing on a place or person.

• Early art that reflects scenes from everyday life, such as the tomb paintings of the ancient Egyptians, can tell us much about how people lived, their clothing, food, culture, and technology.

• Sculpture is another form of art that has existed since the earliest times, from the stylised carved stone statues of Sumer to the lifelike marble figures of ancient Greece, famous for their naturalness, beauty, and perfect proportions.

The first stencils
In many different places—Argentina, Australia, France, and Spain—almost identical prehistoric paintings of hands have been found, even though the people who made them could never have been in contact. It is thought that these paintings were made by the artists blowing paint from their mouths or through tubes of wood or bone to create a stencil of their hand held against the rock face.

CAVE PAINTINGS OF THE STONE AGE

One of the richest discoveries of Ice Age painting is in the Dordogne region of southwest France. Here, in Lascaux, the cave walls are covered with paintings of wild animals—horses, wild boar, as well as aurochs (wild cattle). The outlines were painted by hand using fur brushes and filled in with pigment blown through bone tubes.

The art of fresco

The Minoans are credited with inventing the art of fresco, where pictures are painted directly on to the wet plaster of walls and ceilings. Many palace walls, such as this example from the throne room of the Minoan palace at Knossos, were covered with vivid scenes of palace life and brightly colored depictions of plants and mythical creatures.

Marvelous mosaics

The Romans are well known for their mosaics—pictures created from small pieces of colored glass or stone—which adorned the walls, floors, and ceilings of villas throughout the Roman Empire. The images often included tiny details of people's clothing, hairstyles, or everyday artifacts, as well as scenes such as this view of a gladiator fighting a leopard.

The Sumerians believed that if they placed statues like this in their temples, the statue would pray for them.

A Greek statue of Demeter, goddess of the harvest. The Greeks often placed such statues at the site of shrines where people could make offerings to the gods.

PAINTING MATERIALS

Early artists had few materials to help them with their creations—no pots of paint or packets of felt-tip pens. Instead, they used the resources around them. The main colors used in prehistoric art—yellow, red, brown, and white—came from different types of soil or rock, ground down and mixed with animal fat, blood, or spit to create a kind of paint. Black came from charcoal (burnt wood). The paint was applied using fingertips or pads made of lichen or moss. Twigs could be used to make finer lines and feathers for blending areas of color. Later, animal hair was bound into primitive brushes. and new pigments were invented by grinding up mineral stones.

TOMB PAINTINGS OF THE PHARAOHS

The art of ancient Egypt is characterized by a sense of order, with clear outlines and flat areas of color. Figures were painted with their heads and limbs in profile but their shoulders and eyes facing the viewer. They were also sized according to their importance, so the pharaoh would always be the largest figure in any scene. Egyptian artists covered their tomb walls with a fine layer of plaster, painting on their scenes using reed or wheat heads or frayed sticks bound together into brushes.

MONUMENTS AND MEGALITHS

ONE OF THE MOST REMARKABLE HUMAN ACHIEVEMENTS OF THE PREHISTORIC AGE was our ability to build gigantic monuments out of stone. Even though the people who created them had no help from machines of any sort, they used their growing intelligence and creativity to build massive structures, many of which are still standing today.

During the Megalithic Period, from 9000 BCE to 1300 CE, people in many different parts of the world created these enormous constructions (known as megaliths), for use as tombs, ceremonial sites, temples, or even giant observatories—a monumental way to measure the position of the sun, moon and stars.

This so-called megalithic culture was only possible where humans had settled in communities big enough to support the organization of such ambitious building projects—and reveals that, despite popular belief, the people who built them were anything but primitive.

Stonehenge, southern England, c.3000 BCE

Perhaps the world's most spectacular stone circle, Stonehenge took more than a thousand years to build. It was made out of stones that had been transported over a considerable distance using nothing but ropes, logs, and manpower.

Archaeologists believe the stones (some of which weighed as much as 24 double-decker buses) were raised using a complex system of levers and ropes and were part of a larger prehistoric site, possibly used to glorify the dead or as a giant outdoor calendar.

Deer Stones, Mongolia, c.1000 BCE

The "Ganghwa Dolmens," Korea, c.1000 BCE

Lore Lindu, Indonesia, c.2000 BCE

Nazca Lines, Peru, c.500 BCE

Not all monumental undertakings of the ancient world involved the raising of huge slabs of rock. In the Nazca Desert of southern Peru, another mark of early human achievement was the creation of hundreds of gigantic figures, so enormous in scale that they can be seen from space. They were carved by the Nazca people into the surface of the plateau over an area of 170 square miles (450 square kilometers).

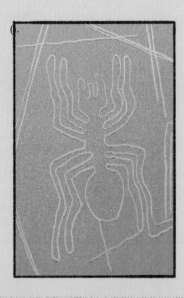

THE FIRST CIVILIZATIONS

IMAGINE MESOPOTAMIA, OVER 7,000 YEARS AGO. Thanks to the advent of farming, people had started to build the first small settlements. Over time, these settlements grew into towns as more and more people arrived to live there, drawn by the reliable source of food and the security of a growing community. Soon, food was so abundant that not everyone needed to farm, so some townspeople had time to learn new skills, such as how to make clay pots or weave cloth. As the towns grew so, their inhabitants developed new ways of organizing themselves, inventing ways of storing and distributing food, new means of protecting themselves from their enemies, and new networks through which they could trade goods.

The towns eventually grew into huge walled cities, each with their own potters and weavers, farmers and builders, rulers, subjects and priests. One such collection of city states belonged to the Sumerians. Uruk, one of their first cities, was home to over 10,000 people. Supported by the farmland of the Fertile Crescent, the city's narrow streets of mud-brick housing were filled with craftworkers making goods that were traded as far away as India and Arabia. At Uruk's center was a great temple where its rulers were buried with their treasures and sometimes with their servants too—who drank poison and lay down to die next to their royal master or mistress.

During the next few thousand years, other cities and civilizations would spring up all over the ancient world. Some became all-powerful, conquering their neighbors to create the first empires. And when those empires collapsed or were taken over by their rivals, they left behind the story of their culture—in their idols and artifacts, their great temples and tombs—which tell us today what life was like in those early cities of long ago.

A SUMERIAN CITY, 3000 BCE

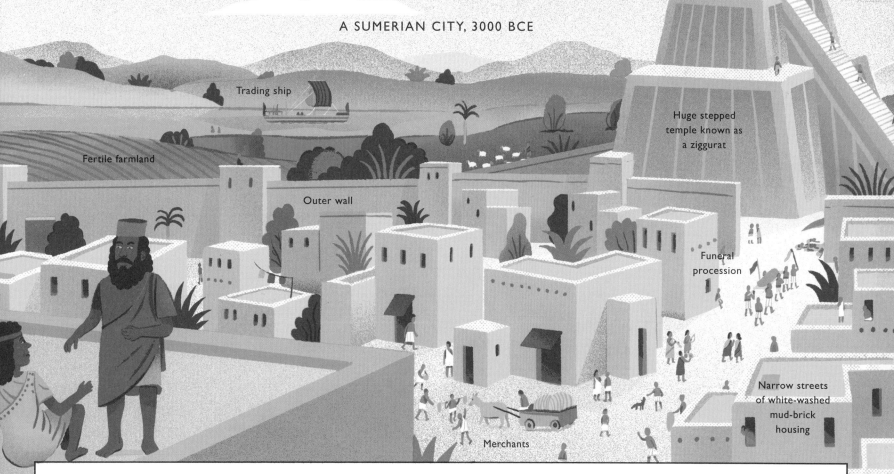

Trading ship

Huge stepped temple known as a ziggurat

Fertile farmland

Outer wall

Funeral procession

Narrow streets of white-washed mud-brick housing

Merchants

Gold items, such as this necklace, were placed in the tombs of Sumerian kings and queens.

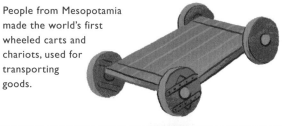

People from Mesopotamia made the world's first wheeled carts and chariots, used for transporting goods.

They also invented the world's first writing system—known as "cuneiform" script.

A BRIEF HISTORY OF JEWELRY

EVER SINCE HUMANS FIRST WALKED THE EARTH, THEY HAVE ADORNED THEMSELVES WITH JEWELRY. Whether as a means of self-expression, to attract a mate or signify status, we will never know—but it is possible that early humans thought of decorating themselves with jewelry even before they thought of making anything resembling clothing.

Today, jewelry is commonly worn in all cultures and at all levels of society, but this wasn't always so. In ancient Rome, for example, only certain ranks could wear rings and various laws dictated who could wear what type of jewelry. Similarly, in the European Middle Ages, the use of jewelry was not common, except among higher nobility and royalty.

Since its first appearance, humans have used jewelry for a number of different reasons:
• For its practical function—generally to fix clothing or hair in place, or to tell the time (in the case of watches).
• As a mark of social or personal status, such as a crown or a wedding ring.
• As a sign of affiliation to an ethnic, religious, or social group—for example, a Christian crucifix or set of tribal beads.
• To provide protection or ward off evil in the form of a talisman—for example, an amulet.
• As a symbol of love, mourning, or even luck.
• As a display of human artistry or creativity.

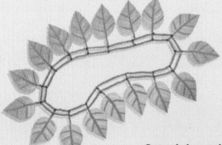

Thracian gold brooch—4400 BCE. The ancient Thracians produced the oldest-known objects made from gold. They lived in southeastern Europe.

Queen Pu-abi's necklace—2600 BCE. When her tomb was found in the 1920s, a Sumerian queen was wearing this necklace of hammered gold and her whole upper body was hung with beads.

Scarab brooch—1323 BCE. This pectoral (a brooch designed to lay on the chest and often worn suspended from a necklace) was part of the Pharaoh Tutankhamun's coronation regalia.

Roman seal ring—500 BCE. Made of gold, seal or signet rings were used to make impressions in soft wax, to authenticate or seal important documents. They often carried the face of the emperor on an inset stone.

PREHISTORIC JEWELRY

These talons would once have been joined to form a bracelet—one of the oldest surviving pieces of jewelry in the world. They tell us that even as far back as the Neanderthals early humans had a need to adorn themselves with ornaments and increasingly had the skills and artistry to do so.

Spiral snake bracelet—400 BCE. Greek jewelry often included animal designs, such as this gold bracelet of two snakes whose tails are tied in a Hercules (also known as a reef or love) knot, and decorated with precious stones.

Viking brooch—900 CE. Cast from bronze and used instead of buttons to fasten clothing, these brooches were so commonly worn that they have been found wherever the Vikings settled.

Eagle-talon bracelet— c135,000 BCE

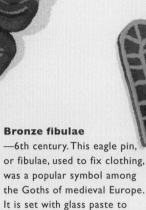

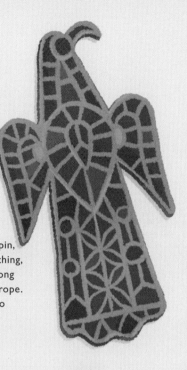

Bear's-teeth necklace
—1st century. The Hopewell culture flourished in North America c.100 BCE. Burial remains discovered in the 1980s included this trophy necklace.

Mochica earspools
—1st century. The Moche people of northern Peru were superb metalworkers. These earspools feature inlays of shell, turquoise, mother of pearl, and amethyst.

Hei-tiki pendant
—2nd century. The hei-tiki, an ornamental pendant worn by the New Zealand Maori, is said to be a sign of fertility.

Bronze fibulae
—6th century. This eagle pin, or fibulae, used to fix clothing, was a popular symbol among the Goths of medieval Europe. It is set with glass paste to imitate garnets.

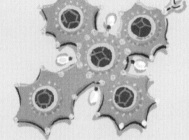

Jade dragon pendant—
500 CE. Chinese jewelry often focused on the use of jade, which was thought to protect the bearer, as well as being a symbol of the grace and morality of the wearer.

Medieval reliquary cross—1400. Within the interior of this cross a secret compartment held a relic—a tiny fragment of a deceased holy person's body or belongings. It was used as a focus for religious meditation.

Diamond engagement ring—1477. In 1477, Archduke Maximillian of Austria commissioned the world's very first diamond engagement ring for his betrothed, Mary of Burgundy.

Aztec lip plug
—15th century. Among the Aztecs, only nobility wore gold jewelry. In general, the more jewelry a noble wore, the higher his status or prestige.

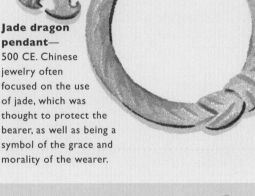

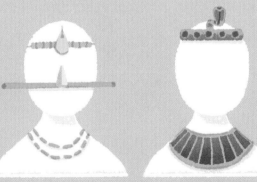

Nose bone—c.44,000 BCE. Worn by indigenous Australians for thousands of years, nose bones were often carved from kangaroo bone. A discovery dating from around 44,000 BCE is the oldest piece of bone jewelry made by man.

Wesekh Collar—1500 BCE. A characteristic form of Egyptian jewelry, the weskhet is a collar composed of cylinders strung in layers around a central choker. A favorite of the pharaohs, it was often made of gold.

Medieval necklace—16th century.
During the Middle Ages, European jewelry design was influenced by the availability of new gemstones, the result of the great explorations of the time.

Masai tribal beads—16th century.
The Masai people of East Africa used clay, wood, bone, copper, and glass to make their distinctive beaded neck discs. They signify age and social status.

Mughal flower bracelet—16th century. This hathphool (meaning "flowers for the hand") from Rajasthan consists of a gem-encrusted bracelet with chains connected to rings for each of the five fingers.

A MATERIAL WORLD

THE WEARING OF CLOTHING IS SPECIFICALLY A HUMAN CHARACTERISTIC, borne from the need to protect ourselves from natural elements like heat, cold, and rain, or from insects or thorny plants. Since the Neanderthals first draped themselves with animal skins, the clothes we have worn and the materials used to make them have changed under the influences of climates, cultures, fashion, wealth, and technological invention.

The first materials used for clothing were animal skins, initially simply tied around the body, then sewn crudely together using bone needles and thread made from animal sinew. With farming came the growing of crops and the domestication of animals and with them our invention of new materials. By weaving or knitting fibers together, we could make not just clothing but many other useful things, from baskets and blankets to rope and sailcloth.

• Linen, made from the fibers of the flax plant, is one of the oldest forms of textile, first seen around 8000 BCE, and highly regarded for its quality and beauty. Apart from its use for clothing, linen was also used in ancient Egypt to make bandages for mummification and for burial shrouds. It was so valued among the Egyptians that it was even used as a form of currency.
• Cotton, made from a fiber that grows around the seed of the cotton plant, has been part of human history for over 7,000 years. The farmers of the Indus Valley were the first people to grow cotton and weave it into cloth.
• Sheep, goats, rabbits, musk ox, camels, vicunas, llamas, and alpacas have all been used to provide wool in different parts of the world. Easy to spin and with fantastic insulating properties, wool was used to make clothing in both very cold and very hot climates.

Soay sheep—some of the earliest woolen clothes in Europe were probably made from the fleeces of sheep like this.

A **charkha**, one of the oldest forms of spinning wheel, invented in India, c.700 CE.

Printed silk from China

Woven woolen cloth from ancient Greece

Indian cotton showing woodblock printing

Embroidered cloth from ancient Peru

Checked wool from Celtic Europe

Handwoven blanket from Central America

Egyptian linen

The technique of **making felt** by rolling, beating, and pressing animal hair or wool into a fabric is older than spinning and weaving. Many cultures have legends about how felt-making was invented. Christians say it was the invention of Saint Christopher, who packed his sandals with wool to prevent blisters and found at the end of his journey that the wool had become felt socks!

Embroidered felt boots from Outer Mongolia, c.900 CE

Nålebound socks from Egypt, c.300 BCE

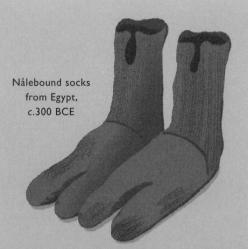

Nålebinding was another early method of making material—a type of knitting made using a single needle—that first appeared around 6500 BCE. The first items of clothing found that used this technique were socks.

Knitting is a technique for making fabric using yarn on two or more needles. The oldest knitted items have been found in Egypt and are dated between the 11th and 14th centuries BCE.

Most histories of knitting place its origins in the Middle East. These gloves were made by Muslim knitters employed by Spanish royalty in the 11th century.

Spinning is an ancient textile art in which plant or animal fibers are drawn out and twisted together to form yarn. In the most primitive type of spinning, tufts of animal hair or plant fiber are rolled down the thigh with the hand. Later, the fiber was spun using simple tools, the spindle and distaff, and on various kinds of spinning wheel.

Cotton "bolls" showing the plant fibers that can be spun into yarn.

Flax plant—the stems were soaked (retted) to separate the hard parts from the fibers useful for spinning.

Spindle and distaff wound with linen yarn.

Woven mummy bandage from the tomb of Tutankhamen

The ability to weave two separate strands of yarn or thread together to form fabric marked a great step forward in human history. In **weaving**, a set of longer threads (the warp) are interlaced with a set of crossing threads (the weft) to form cloth. This is done on a frame known as a loom of which there are a number of different types.

Ancient Egyptians using a hand loom

THE LEGEND OF SILK

Mulberry silk moth (Bombyx mori) with its caterpillar and cocoon

Ladies folding silk during the Han dynasty

Legend has it that silk was discovered by the wife of the Yellow Emperor of China over 4,000 years ago. She realized that the cocoons of certain moths could be unraveled and turned into yarn. When woven, they created a soft, light, but incredibly strong fabric that was to play an important role in the culture and economy of China for thousands of years.

• The moths used for silk-making were reared in captivity and the Chinese planted whole forests of mulberry trees on which to rear the caterpillars.
• The Chinese kept the art of making silk a secret for over 1,000 years—anyone caught revealing the secret was put to death. Eventually two monks from the Byzantine Empire smuggled some silkworm eggs

out of China in their walking sticks and the ability to make silk spread to other countries.
• Silk was highly prized in ancient China and wearing it was an important status symbol. It was such a valuable export that the main trading routes between the East and West became commonly known as the Silk Road.

CULTURE AND

FROM EARLIEST TIMES, DIFFERENT CULTURES AND CIVILIZATIONS HAVE CREATED THEIR OWN PARTICULAR WAY OF DRESSING. They made use of the resources around them to design clothing and other adornments that suited the climate in which they lived, the jobs people had to do, or that reflected their status in society. Although many cultures had access to similar materials, they interpreted their use in myriad ways, each adding to the rich history of clothing and costume that still influences the fashions of today.

A. Neolithic hunter, c.4000 BCE
In the Stone Age, most clothing was made of leather, fur, or woven grasses. The hunters of the last Ice Age were probably the first people to wear recognizable clothes instead of just draping or tying skins around their bodies.

B. Egyptian finery, 1500 BCE
The ancient Egyptians needed cool, light material to make clothing suitable for their hot, dry climate, and the answer was linen. Unlike other cultures that lived alongside them, the Egyptians preferred to sew their clothes to fit their bodies rather than swathing themselves in draped lengths of material. Both men and women wore tight-fitting tunics and men often wore a wrap-around skirt that was tied at the waist with a belt. The length of the skirt varied depending on fashion—and in the time of the New Kingdom, it was fashionable to wear pleats! Clothes were often highly decorative and complemented by the use of lots of jewelry, worn by both men and women. The type and quality of material used reflected the wealth of the wearer and people of importance often wore specific items to denote their status.

C. Persian style, c.500 BCE
The ancestors of the Persians were horse-riding nomads who inhabited the icy Asian steppes, so unsurprisingly they developed clothes that were warm and comfortable to wear. Most Persian clothes were sewn and fitted to the body and made from wool, linen, and, later, silk.

D. Colorful Celts, c.400 BCE
The Celts loved bright colors and often dyed their wool before weaving it into colorful patterns. They continued to wear furs long after weaving was invented, draping fur capes around themselves for warmth or wearing fur waistcoats over woolen tunics.

A

Goatskin coat stitched with sinew

Deerhide boots stuffed with hay

Leopard skin shows priesthood

B

Eye makeup

C

Leather shoes tied to feet with laces

D

Trousers of checked wool

Braided hair

Wool cloak doubles as blanket

Gold fibulae

E

Linen tunic

Woolen tunic

Leather sandal

COSTUME

E. Graceful Greeks, c.400 BCE
During the Classical Period of ancient Greece, most people wore graceful, draped clothing, often made of wool and consisting of various different types of tunic and cloak pinned together with brooches called fibulae.

F. Roman rules c.100 CE
Many Roman clothes were influenced by styles from regions that had been conquered and become part of the Roman Empire, especially the Greek forms of dress. The most important item in the ancient Roman wardrobe was the toga—a one-piece woolen garment that could be wrapped around the body in different ways, There were strict rules about who could wear certain styles of dress—during the time of the Republic, only

Roman citizens could wear togas for example, and only the emperor or his consuls could wear a purple one.

G. Ancient China, c.200 BCE
Silk was the favored fabric of the wealthy in ancient China, where clothes were an essential part of the wearer's social status. Rich and poor dressed differently—the poor using clothes made of hemp, which were durable and comfortable to work in, padded sometimes for warmth. Only the rich wore silk, often dyed or embroidered with intricate designs, and only an emperor could dress in yellow. White clothing was worn during mourning (when someone died), and red was worn to show joy and happiness. Styles of clothing changed with the different

dynasties—the robe shown here is the traditional dress of the Han dynasty, worn by men and women.

H. Feathery fashions, c.400 CE
The Mayans made colorful clothing of light materials that suited their hot climate. Important people had clothes of woven cotton stained with plant dyes, often decorated with embroidery, feathers, or shells, while the poor used fibers from sisal (a type of plant now used to make rope).

I. Mauryan India, c.200 BCE
During the Mauryan era, both men and women wore loincloths, fastened in a knot at the center of the waist. Another cloth could be tied around the hips to form a skirt. On top, both men and women wore a long scarf that could be worn in several ways.

COLORFUL CLOTH

Colorful, decorated clothing is a feature of many cultures—yarn stained in different colors and then woven into elaborate patterns, or embellished with embroidery, beads, or shells.

For at least 100,000 years, humans have known how to create dyes from the natural resources around them. Dyes from plant sources were the most common—madder root for red, lichen for yellow, indigo for blue—but the most precious dye of the ancient world was royal purple obtained by "milking" the secretions from the murex sea snail.

Gold wreath

Long hair tied into a topknot

Feathered headdress

Ear-spools

Turban

G

F

Gold net ring

Padded jacket

Wide sleeves

H

I

Loincloth

Royal purple toga

Trousers of rough hemp or cotton

Silk slippers with curled toes

Leather sandals with closed back

Gold ankle hoops

THE DISCOVERY OF METAL

AROUND 5,000 YEARS AGO, HUMANS DISCOVERED HOW TO MAKE METAL. Before this, the only metals we used were nuggets of copper, gold, or silver—soft metals that could be beaten into shape to make different things. Then we found that if you heated up certain kinds of rock—ones containing metal ore—molten metal would pour out. This is called smelting.

One of the first metals to be smelted was copper. It could be hammered to make pots and pans and fancy jewelry, but it was too soft to make hard-wearing tools or weapons. After a couple of thousand years of experimenting, metalworkers in Egypt and Mesopotamia discovered that by adding tin to copper at high temperatures they could form a much stronger

metal called bronze. So began the Bronze Age, an era in human evolution that happened in different places at different times as the knowledge of how to make bronze spread from its origins in the Middle East, or as civilizations (such as those in ancient China) made the discovery for themselves. The Bronze Age was followed by a time when people learned to smelt and shape iron ore to produce even stronger tools and weapons, during a period known as the Iron Age.

The discovery of metals played a key role in shaping the human world. It provided us with strong, long-lasting materials that could be used to make a wide variety of objects, from weapons of war and pieces of armor to cooking utensils and ornaments.

Selection of Iron Age artifacts, northern Europe, c.600 BCE

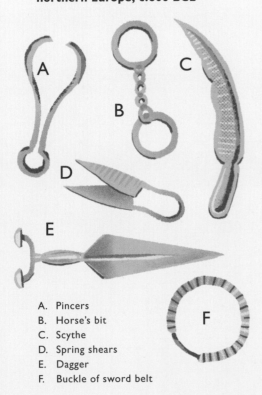

A. Pincers
B. Horse's bit
C. Scythe
D. Spring shears
E. Dagger
F. Buckle of sword belt

Hammered copper objects from Mohenjo-daro, c.2000 BCE, one of the largest settlements of the Indus Valley civilization.

Iron and bronze sword, c.900 BCE

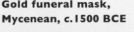

Iron Age hair pin, c.600 BCE

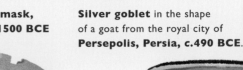

Bronze cauldron, Shang China, c.1650 BCE, used for cooking, storage, and offerings to the gods.

Gold funeral mask, Mycenean, c.1500 BCE

Silver goblet in the shape of a goat from the royal city of **Persepolis, Persia, c.490 BCE.**

8000 BCE
The first type of metalwork emerges, involving the **hammering** of raw nuggets of gold and copper.

5500 BCE
Copper smelting (heating ore to extract pure metal) starts in the Middle East.

3200 BCE
Metal-casting Using molds and molten metal to form objects begins in Mesopotamia.

3000 BCE
The creation of **bronze** becomes widespread in the great city-based civilizations of Egypt and Mesopotamia.

2000 BCE
The knowledge of **bronze-working** spreads to the Minoans and Mycenians of the Aegean region.

1900 BCE
Iron Age starts in western Asia.

1800 BCE
Bronze Age reaches Eastern Europe.

MAKING METAL

Smelting—People learned to extract metal from ore by heating the rocks that contained it. First they heated the ore to a high temperature. When the metal in the ore reached melting point, they collected it in round crucibles made of stone. The metal could then be used to make useful or decorative objects.

Casting—Bronze Age people made all sorts of objects by pouring molten metals into stone molds, a process known as casting. Once the metal had cooled and set, the mold was opened to reveal the finished item. On the right you can see a bronze decorative figure and its stone mold from Mesopotamia, **c.**1800 BCE.

THE TRADE IN TIN

To make bronze, you need a good supply of copper and tin, but although they had access to plenty of copper ore, tin was not so common in ancient Egypt and Mesopotamia. To rectify the problem, new trade networks were created to bring in tin from outlying regions thousands of miles away, such as Cornwall in the British Isles and the so-called Ore Mountains of Central Europe. By 1250 BCE, the trade network in tin stretched outward from the great city-based Middle Eastern civilizations across the whole of eastern and northern Europe.

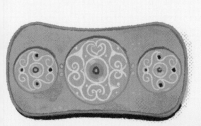

The Battersea Shield, c.350 BCE. Found in the River Thames, this Celtic shield is made of sheet bronze inlaid with studs of red glass and attached to a wooden backing.

Bronze gladiator helmet, Rome, 100 CE, found at the gladiatorial barracks in Pompeii.

Mochica mask from Peru, c.800 CE, made from copper and gold with eyes of shell. Although the Moche civilizations lasted for 1,000 years, they never produced iron.

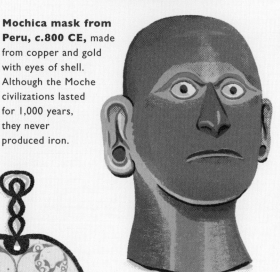

Iron Age mirror, c.50 BCE, Britain, made from bronze with a cast handle. The back of the polished reflecting plate has intricate engraving.

Carved copper bird, Hopewell tribe, North America, c.200 BCE

Benin bronze figures, 16th century. Craft-workers from the Kingdom of Benin (present-day Nigeria) made beautiful cast-bronze figures.

1650 BCE
Bronze casting begins in Shan China.

1300 BCE
Furnaces with bellows are created in Egypt, which provide the higher temperatures necessary for **iron smelting.**

800 BCE
Iron Age starts in central Europe.

100 BCE
The **blast furnace** is invented in China—used for making iron cooking pots and tools.

METALWORKING TIMELINE

ANOTHER BRICK IN THE WALL...

The oldest walls found in existence are those of the Temple of Göbekli Tepe in Turkey, dateing to 11,500 years ago. The massive carved stones were arranged by prehistoric people who had not yet developed metal tools or even pottery.

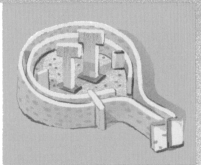

Maiden Castle in Dorset, England, is one of the largest Iron Age hill forts in Europe—the size of 50 football fields. Its huge ramparts once protected hundreds of residents, part of a defensive sytem built by the Celts in an effort to hold back the spread of the Roman Empire.

FROM EARLY HISTORY, WALLS HAVE BEEN A FEATURE OF MOST HUMAN SETTLEMENTS. Even before they were used in houses, groups of humans were protecting their homes by building walled defenses around them.

The word "wall" comes from the Latin *vallus*, meaning "stake" and originally referred to the wood-stake and earth fences that formed the outer edge of many early fortifications. As settlements got bigger, walls were used to mark the borders of cities and later still to mark the territorial boundaries of empires. Walls were also important as symbols—showing visitors that the people who built them were powerful and independent.

• The city of Jericho (now in the West Bank) was one of the first cities to be surrounded by defensive walls in around the 10th century BCE, along with the later city of Uruk.

• King Hammurabi, founder of the Babylonian Empire, surrounded his city with impressive walls over 3,500 years ago, but it took another thousand years for them to be transformed into a true wonder of the ancient world by King Nebuchadnezzar II. He built not just one but three walls around Babylon, at heights of nearly 40 feet (12 meters) or more and so broad that chariots could race on top of them.

• Hadrian's Wall, one of Europe's most famous ancient walls, was built across the northern border of Roman Britain by the emperor Hadrian to keep out the invading Picts. It took six years to build, stretched for 80 miles (128 kilometers) between what is now England and Scotland and was, at points, over 19 feet (6 meters) high and nearly 9 feet (3 meters) wide. It had towers along its length and served as a symbol of Roman military might and power.

The Ishtar Gate in the wall of Nebuchadnezzar II's Babylon was claimed by some to be greater than any of the Wonders of the ancient World (see page 55). Dedicated to the goddess Ishtar, the gate was made of glazed brick covered in lapis lazuli, a deep-blue semiprecious stone, and decorated with beautiful designs.

A SECTION OF THE GREAT WALL BEING BUILT DURING THE MING DYNASTY

Lookout tower

Stone paving

Peasant workers

Bamboo scaffolding

Soil and rubble

Overseer

Stone slabs

THE GREAT WALL OF CHINA

PERHAPS THE MOST FAMOUS WALL IN THE WORLD, the Great Wall of China stretches for 13,000 miles (21,000 kilometers) along what used to be the northern border of China, passing over steep mountainsides, through deserts and thick forests. The wall was made up of a series of different fortifications—of stone, brick, rammed earth, wood, and other materials—and was originally started under China's first emperor around 200 BCE. He ordered the joining together of smaller walls erected by earlier rulers and extended the wall to form a defense against invasion by the nomadic tribes that roamed the Asian steppes. Peasants and criminals were used to supply the hard labor needed and any worker that died on the job had his body buried within the wall itself. It is estimated that over a million people died during the wall's construction. The wall was not completed until the time of the Ming dynasty (1368–1644) and still stands today as the biggest man-made structure in the world.

LIVING FROM THE LAND

THE PRACTICE OF FARMING, OR AGRICULTURE, DEVELOPED OVER THOUSANDS OF YEARS, FROM ITS BEGINNINGS OVER 12,000 YEARS AGO. Over time, farmers were able to develop crops from the wild plants that grew around them and domesticate wild animals such as sheep and cattle, breeding them to produce a ready supply of meat, milk, wool, leather, and bone. They invented tools to help them farm, systems of irrigation to take water to where it was needed most, and they also learned how to fertilize soil so yet more land could be used for farming. As farming became more efficient, less of the population needed to be involved in the production of food and could specialize instead in developing other useful skills, such as weaving or metalwork.

EARLY TOOLS

The very first farmers didn't use many tools to help them. They poked holes in the ground with sticks to plant seeds and did most of their work using their bare hands. But human ingenuity soon lead to the creation of the first farming tools Teosintehoes to work the soil, sickles to cut the grain for harvesting, grinding stones and axes.

At first, these tools were fashioned from sharpened flints attached to wooden handles, but in around 3000 BCE, people in Egypt and Mesopotamia learned how to make bronze by mixing tin and copper. This new metal, and the discovery of iron some 1,000 years later, meant that farmers had an increasing array of tools to help them improve their farming.

Another big step forward came with the introduction of the plow. Plows were made of a piece of wood, later tipped with metal, pulled at first by hand and later by one or two oxen. In Mesopotamia, pictographs from around 4000 BCE show early plows being used to make a groove called a furrow in the earth. Working the soil like this brought nutrients to the surface, helping the seeds scattered in the furrow to grow.

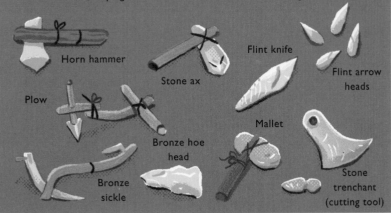

Horn hammer
Stone ax
Flint knife
Flint arrow heads
Plow
Mallet
Bronze hoe head
Bronze sickle
Stone trenchant (cutting tool)

WILD BEGINNINGS

All farm animals and crops are descended from wild species that have been changed by selective breeding over thousands of years—a process known as "domestication." Early farmers would sow only the seeds of plants that yielded the largest grains or the most plentiful crop, and breed from animals that provided a useful resource—for their hide, wool, or meat and, later, that could be tamed to pull plows or carry grain.

Aurochs—Cow   Mouflon—Sheep   Wild boar—Pig

Einkorn—Wheat   Teosinte—Maize

FIRE-STICK FARMING

A quite different method of farming was practiced by the indigenous Australians, perhaps as long as 50,000 years ago. They regularly used fire to burn vegetation, firstly to make hunting easier, as the fires themselves would flush out small game that could then be more easily hunted down. Secondly, fire-stick farming could change the makeup of plant and animal species in an area to a human's advantage. Over time, it turned dry forest into savanna, thereby increasing the population of grass-eating species like the kangaroo, an important source of food, and edible ground-level plants like bush potatoes and water chestnuts.

ROW-CROP FARMING

The Chinese invented row-crop farming to make crops like rice and wheat easier to harvest. Planting seeds in rows rather than scattering them randomly provided a ready walkway through the crops. This made it easier to irrigate the fields and caused less damage to the crops when harvesting took place.

FARMING ON A GRAND SCALE

A civilization can only thrive when its people have a secure supply of food. The success of their agriculture was the principle reason for the great achievements of the ancient Egyptians. They were the first large-scale farmers, largely thanks to the fertile soil that existed along the edge of the River Nile. This allowed them to grow crops, such as wheat, barley, pomegranates, vines, and also flax for linen. In addition to hand tools, they also had ox-drawn plows and a sophisticated system of irrigation canals to help water the land.

This tomb painting from ancient Egypt shows a farmer using his ox-drawn plow to cut furrows in the earth. His wife would follow behind to scatter the seeds.

Pivot

C

A

Counterweight

C

B

D

E

F

Irrigation channel

THE FARMING YEAR

Akhet
The Inundation
(June to September)

Peret
The Growing Season
(October to February)

Shemu
The Harvest
(March to May)

KEY TO PLATE

A. This ancient Egyptian invention is called a **shaduf**. Made of a bucket attached to a long weighted pole, it was used to lift water from the river into an irrigation channel that fed the fields.
B. **Sickles** first of sharpened flint and then bronze were used to harvest wheat.
C. **Ditches** and **canals** stored and carried floodwater to the crops.

D. The wheat is carried away in **papyrus baskets**.
E. Cows were used to trample the wheat, separating the grain from the stalks (a process known as **threshing**).
F. The grain was tossed to separate it from the hard outside shell or husk (a process known as **winnowing**) before it was stored in specially built grain stores.

During the growing and harvesting seasons, the farmers of ancient Egypt were busy—planting, plowing, and gathering crops. When the land flooded during the rainy season, the farmers spent their time making tools or worked for the pharaoh building pyramids and temples.

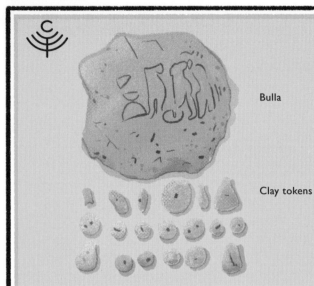

Clay tokens and "envelope," Mediterranean, 6000 BCE

Writing numbers for the purpose of record-keeping began long before the writing of language and became even more important with the advent of farming. Small clay tokens in simple shapes—cones, spheres, cylinders—that were then incised with lines or dots were made as long ago as 7500 BCE. The tokens represented different goods—jars of oil, livestock, measures of grain—and recorded when materials had been bought or sold. The Sumerians even invented clay "envelopes," called bulla, in which to encase their tokens, marking the exterior with the shapes of the tokens inside—the first step toward the more complex forms of writing that followed.

Bulla

Clay tokens

Limestone tablet from Sumer, c.3500 BCE
This carved stone tablet from the Sumerian city of Kish shows early pictographs—perhaps the earliest known example of writing.

THE ORIGINS OF WRITING

WRITING IS ONE OF THE GREATEST OF ALL HUMAN INVENTIONS. It provides a tool by which we can store and communicate knowledge, in greater detail than could ever be achieved by the spoken word. The ability to write allows us to share information across time and space—capturing the words of a prophet, engraving the tombstone of a pharaoh, or simply keeping a record of taxes owed.

The introduction of a writing system marks an important point in the evolution of any civilization because it allows people not only to communicate over great distances, but also to communicate beyond their own time. Much of our knowledge of the ancient world comes from texts left behind by these long-lost peoples, and it is only with the advent of writing that we consider the history of any culture to have begun.
• Writing developed independently in various parts of the world at about the same time as people began to live in communities. The ancient peoples of the Middle East, China, and South America all separately invented their own systems of writing to record and present information too complex to rely on human memory

alone. One of the oldest examples of writing is concerned with recording the daily ration of beer given to each citizen!
• Some of the first examples of writing date from about 5,000 years ago and were made by the Sumerians of Mesopotamia. Like many early writing systems, they used pictorial symbols as a way of recording information about objects and numbers.
• The problem with many early writing systems was that they required the memorization of hundreds of different symbols, or pictographs. The next breakthrough in the history of writing came with the recognition that all words are composed of sound units and can therefore be represented with symbols for those sounds—in other words, an alphabet.
• The world's first alphabet was invented by the Phoenicians, based on 22 symbols that corresponded with the sounds of the spoken language, but it only had letters for consonants. It was the ancient Greeks that added symbols for the vowel sounds in around 1000 BCE, and it is from this first alphabet that all the alphabets of the Western world have evolved—including the Roman alphabet we use today.

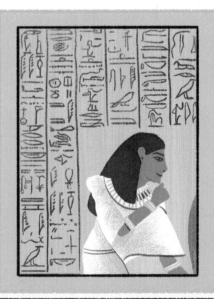

Page from the Egyptian *Book of the Dead* c.1250 BCE
Around the same time as cuneiform script appeared, the Egyptians invented their own form of writing. Now known as hieroglyphics, it used over 700 different picture signs that corresponded to sounds or words.

They carved these hieroglyphs into their stone monuments and tomb walls, but they also had other scripts that were written by their priests on papyrus or cloth using reed pens or brushes.

Page from a Mayan Codex, c.900 CE, showing glyphs
Of the various writing systems developed in Mesoamerica, the one that was best developed was Mayan script, which used pictograms or glyphs as symbols for sounds and whole words. The pictograms were written into a special book called a codex, which consisted of paper made out of bark, folded into a concertina.

Cuneiform writing
By 3000 BCE, the Sumerians had developed a form of writing called cuneiform, which literally means "wedge-shaped." It was made by using a simple hand tool to impress triangular marks into wet clay tablets that were then baked hard. Variations of cuneiform were used by many civilizations of the Middle East for over 3,000 years.

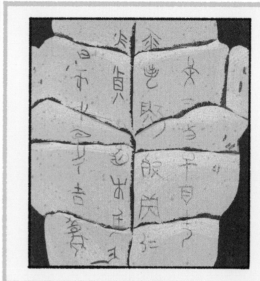

Oracle bone from Shang China
In China the earliest known writing was "oracle bone" script, made during the Shang dynasty c.1400 BCE. Priests posed questions to the gods by scratching them into pieces of tortoiseshell or bone. The inscribed object was then burned in a fire until it cracked. Then the priests "read" the patterns made by the cracks as omens of good or evil.

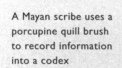

A Mayan scribe uses a porcupine quill brush to record information into a codex

• The written languages of the East all come from Chinese script that was invented independently perhaps as long as 8,000 years ago. The Chinese writing system evolved from a pictographic form and does not have an alphabet. Instead, it uses characters, as many as 50,000, to represent one or more syllables, meanings, objects, pronunciations, or ideas.
• Over time, humans have used many different writing materials. Long before paper was invented, we were making marks in soft clay or wax, carving them on wood, slate, stone or bone or on parchment (the prepared skin of animals).
• Despite the fact that writing was invented over 5,000 years ago, it is only in the last 150 years that most people in the world have been able to read and write. Until then these skills were mainly the preserve of clerics (priests). Even the wealthy were often illiterate and had their own scribes to do their reading and writing for them.

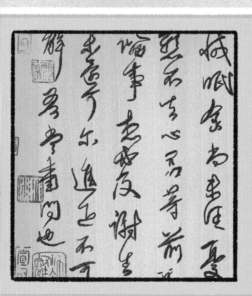

The invention of paper
In around 200 BCE, the Chinese Han dynasty invented paper by leaving a thin layer of pulped tree bark, plants, and rags to dry on a bamboo screen. Before that, silk had often been used as a medium for both writing and painting. The art of writing (calligraphy) was considered a very important skill in ancient China and they made beautiful carved pots to hold their ink, brushes, and water.

Illuminated manuscripts
In the Middle Ages, monks were some of the few people that could read or write. They made handwritten books called manuscripts, usually on religious subjects, beautifully decorated with pictures and patterns and embellished with gold and silver. Most were written in Latin on vellum (a high-quality form of parchment made from calf skin).

The earliest known **scissors** come from Mesopotamia. They were made over 3,000 years ago of two blades connected by a flexible strip of bronze that allowed them to be squeezed together.

The oldest oil **lamp** was found in a cave inhabited over 10,000 years ago. Made from a hollowed-out rock, it likely contained moss soaked in animal fat that, once ignited, burned with a flame. Early pottery lamps like this featured a spout and handle.

The Egyptians developed the first wicked **candle** by dipping rolled papyrus in melted beeswax. Many other early civilizations also developed wicked candles, using everything from insects, tree nuts, and the fruit of the cinnamon tree to make wax.

Whenever you lock your door at night, say a quick thank-you to the ancient Egyptians for inventing the first **door lock**. Created around 4000 BCE, it was made entirely of wood, key included, and involved a system of pegs that held a wooden bar in place. When the key was turned, it released the pegs, allowing the bar to be moved and the door to be opened. This ancient lock is very similar to the locks that most of us have in our houses today, except the key was nearly 12 inches long!

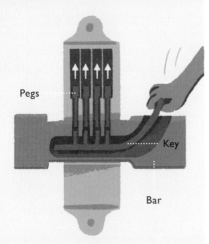

Pegs

Key

Bar

A soap-like material discovered in clay containers during the excavation of Babylon shows that humans have been making **soap** for at least 5,000 years. This soap was made from cassia oil combined with wood ash and water, although it is likely that the substance was used to wash wool and cotton rather than human skin. By 1550 BCE, the Egyptians were making soap from oils and alkaline salts to produce a substance used for treating skin diseases as well as washing.

THE INVENTION OF EVERYDAY THINGS

YOU MAY WELL KNOW THAT HUMANS IN THE ANCIENT WORLD were responsible for many amazing inventions that have shaped our world, like clocks, looms, and furnaces. However, you might be surprised to learn that lots of other, more everyday things that we take for granted today also had their origins many thousands of years ago!

As early as 3000 BCE, the Egyptians were making **paper** from papyrus plants, weaving long strips of pith together before weighting them down to bind them into strong, thin sheets. They also made pens of cut reeds, and mixed soot with beeswax and vegetable gum to make ink. Some 2,000 years later, the Chinese started making paper as we know it from wood pulp.

Egyptian physicians were no strangers to the idea of **false teeth**. More than one mummy has been found where loose teeth had been reattached using gold or silver wire. This dental work may have been done to tidy up the appearance of the corpse for the afterlife!

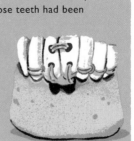

Some ancient inventions were all about having fun. This child's **toy** and **board game**, both made of clay, were excavated from Mohenjo-daro, one of the world's first cities and part of the Indus Valley civilization.

The amazingly durable substance known as *opus caementicium,* or Roman **concrete**, first emerged some 2,100 years ago. It was made by mixing limestone with volcanic ash to form a mortar, and then adding chunks of rock. It was used in the making of roads, bridges, aqueducts, and such famous buildings as the Colosseum.

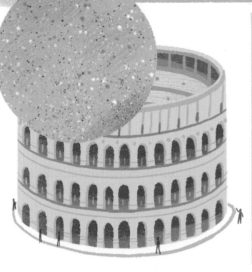

Anaximander, an ancient Greek philosopher, is credited with creating one of the first **maps** of the then known world, c.530 BCE. It showed all the lands grouped around the Aegean Sea with everything surrounded by water.

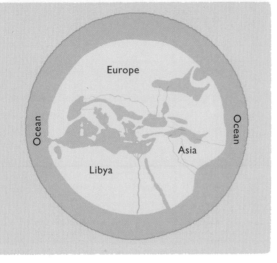

Europe

Ocean

Ocean

Asia

Libya

KEEPING CLEAN

MANY ANCIENT CULTURES HAD WAYS OF KEEPING THEMSELVES CLEAN, BUT IT IS THE ROMANS WHO ARE MOST FAMOUS FOR BUILDING BATHS. Every town had its own bath for the use of citizens, luxuriously appointed with mirrored walls, mosaic floors, pools lined with marble, and water piped in from the surrounding countryside using a complex system of pipes and channels. The baths were a place to go to meet friends as well as to get clean. Only the very rich had private baths in their own homes. Here are some other interesting facts about keeping clean in the ancient world:

• The Celts had written laws governing bathing and personal grooming and had to bathe every Saturday.

They used grooming tools, such as bone combs, tweezers, and ear spoons for cleaning the wax out of their ears!

• The ancient Greeks invented the first sinks and were also the first people to have showers.

• The Egyptians made deodorant by molding fragrant material into pellets that they stored in their armpits. They also frayed the ends of twigs to make toothbrushes.

• Toothsticks, or miswaks, made from the roots of the arak tree (which has antiseptic properties) are still used in Africa and the Middle East today.

• The world's oldest-known recipe for toothpaste comes from ancient Egypt and consists of a mixture of dried iris flower, salt, pepper, and mint.

KEY TO PLATE
A. **Cold-water tank**
B. **Hot-water cylinders**
C. **Fire**
D. **Boiler room**
E. **Slave**
F. **Hypercaust**
(central heating system)
G. **Hot water**
H. **Caldarium** (hot room)
I. **Latrines** (toilets)
J. **Mosaics**
K. **Tepidarium** (warm room)
L. **Cold water**
M. **Frigidarium** (cold room)
N. **Changing room**

HOW TO TAKE A ROMAN BATH:
First take off all your clothes.
Then relax for a while in the Tepidarium.
Now go into the Caldarium. The steam in the room will make you sweat and a slave will rub you all over with perfumed oil.

Next enter the Frigidarium, where another slave will scrape off the sweat and oil, along with any dirt, with an instrument called a strigil.
Now jump into the cold-water pool of the Frigidarium and you're done!

A TYPICAL ROMAN BATH COMPLEX

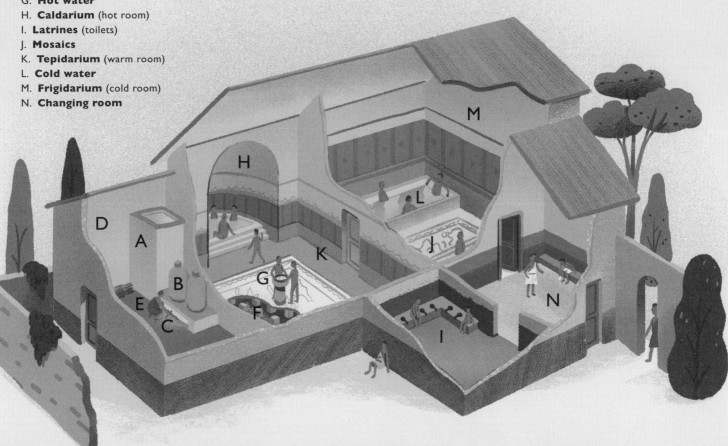

LAWS FOR LIVING

The invention of written language enabled rulers of the ancient world to create laws. The best known of these is the Code of Hammurabi, written by the Babylonian king around 1750 BCE. One of the most well-known of these laws was "an eye for an eye, a tooth for a tooth." Surgeons might have their hand cut off in retribution for a patient dying during an operation, or if a man broke the bone of one of his equals, then his own bone would be broken in return. The laws were carved onto twelve stone pillars and displayed publicly for all to see.

THE ROLE OF RELIGION

In many cultures, religion played a central role in the way society was governed. In the Islamic Empire, people had to live their lives according to Islamic law, which included rules on how they should live, what they could eat and drink and how and when they should pray. In Aztec and Inca society, the high priest wielded almost as much power as the emperor, and in medieval Europe, the head of the Catholic church, the pope (shown below), was more powerful than many kings.

RULES AND RULERS

FROM THE EARLIEST TIMES, AND IN EVERY CULTURE, HUMANS HAVE ORGANIZED THEMSELVES INTO GROUPS, OR COMMUNITIES, AND ESTABLISHED RULES BY WHICH THEY LIVE. Societies needed strong leaders to help protect them from their enemies, and who would set the rules and codes of conduct by which people lived.

Many ancient civilizations were ruled by a single individual. In Mesopotamia, each city was run by a group of noblemen, but in times of war, they chose a leader who ruled until the war was over. The wars were so frequent that the leaders eventually became kings, ruling for life and passing down power to their sons. The Egyptians had their pharaohs; India, China, and Rome their emperors; and the medieval kingdoms of Europe their kings and queens. But these powerful leaders couldn't rule alone. They needed strong armies to protect their empires, and sometimes governments to help set and maintain laws. Many relied on armies or a class of nobles to help them maintain their power, but sometimes their most trusted supporters would turn against them, and history is full of tales of the power struggles that followed.

Pharaoh
(Rameses II—
ancient Egypt)

Sultan
(Osman I—
Ottoman
Empire)

King
(Charlemagne—
Medieval Europe)

Emperor
(Qin Shi Huang—
ancient China)

Emperor
(Augustus Caesar—
Roman Empire)

A VOTE FOR DEMOCRACY

The city-states of ancient Greece were some of the first societies to practice democracy—where the government is voted for by the people. In Athens, all free men had a say in how their city was run and the leading politicians would take turns addressing the assembled citizens in open-air theaters before voting took place. This was done by voters scratching their chosen politician's name onto pieces of broken pottery called ostraka. Law and democracy was also at the heart of Viking society, where individual clans had a chief and a council to assist him, but all laws were made and voted on by the free men of each clan.

MILITARY MIGHT

In many societies, the rulers were also skilled soldiers, given the task of protecting their people and lands from invasion. The pharaohs of Egypt led their armies into battle both to protect and expand their empires. The military leaders of ancient Rome often became emperors as a result of their successful conquests, and the Mongol warrior Temujin built his empire by bringing all the nomadic Mongol tribes under his control. His people renamed him Genghis Khan, which means "supreme ruler."

CLASS SYSTEMS

In most ancient civilizations, society was divided into a number of classes. In almost all cases, at the top of the pile were the rich and, at the bottom, the poor—even though they were usually the greatest proportion of the population. Different societies had different criteria to decide who belonged to which class, and there were often laws that stated what classes were allowed to do, wear or even eat.

CASTE SYSTEM

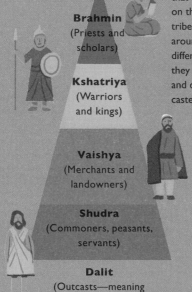

- Gods
- **Brahmin** (Priests and scholars)
- **Kshatriya** (Warriors and kings)
- **Vaishya** (Merchants and landowners)
- **Shudra** (Commoners, peasants, servants)
- **Dalit** (Outcasts—meaning "out of caste")

Caste system

In India, religion defined a social hierarchy that still exists today in some areas. Based on the teaching of the Aryans, the ancient tribes who spread throughout India from around 1500 BCE, people were divided into different classes according to the jobs that they did. You could never change your caste and children always belonged to the same caste as their parents.

Roman society

The seating levels in Rome's great Colosseum were a reflection of social class. The rich and important people sat at the front; the poor sat at the back; and the emperor had a private box for himself and important guests. Slaves were not allowed to attend unless they were there to serve their masters or were being made to fight in the arena.

ROMAN SOCIETY

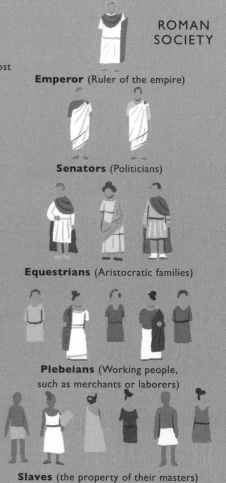

- **Emperor** (Ruler of the empire)
- **Senators** (Politicians)
- **Equestrians** (Aristocratic families)
- **Plebeians** (Working people, such as merchants or laborers)
- **Slaves** (the property of their masters)

CRIME AND PUNISHMENT

Different societies had different attitudes toward what constituted a crime, as well as the most suitable punishment. Some acts, such as murder or theft, were considered crimes in all ancient and medieval societies, but there was huge variation in almost everything else!

- In Aztec society, it was forbidden for the general population to even look at members of the royal family (who were often carried around on a kind of handheld carriage called a litter through the city streets). If they did, they could be put to death.
- The Romans were among the first to use prisons as a form of punishment. One of the most notable was the Mamertine Prison, which was located within a sewer system beneath ancient Rome and contained a large network of dungeons where prisoners were held in squalid conditions.
- One common form of punishment in many societies was to be sentenced to slavery. If you were lucky, that could mean a life as a servant; if you were unlucky, it could mean years of hard labor or being sent to certain death in battle.

- In Viking societies, those accused of a crime had to walk across hot coals or put their hand into boiling water. In this "trial by fire," the individual was deemed innocent if the burns healed.
- In medieval societies, many lesser crimes were punished in public in order to humiliate and disgrace the offenders, and as a warning to others not to misbehave. Being dunked in the village pond on a ducking stool or locked overnight in the stocks were both used to punish misdeeds such as swearing, drunkenness, brawling, and stealing.
- In medieval times, the punishment for people who spoke out against the church was far more serious. They were branded as heretics and often burned to death at the stake. Anyone accused of treason (attempting to overthrow the government or monarchy) was almost always put to death in a particularly drawn-out and painful way.

GODS AND MONSTERS

EVERY HUMAN CULTURE HAS PRACTICED SOME FORM OF RELIGION—an organized system of belief that plays a major role in people's lives. In ancient times, most religions involved the worship of a collection of gods rather than just one. If you wanted to win in battle, you would make offerings to the god of war; for success in matters of the heart, you would pray to the goddess of love. Every culture developed its own different beliefs in these supernatural beings to help explain the world around them—the movement of the stars across the heavens, the changing seasons, or the extremes of weather and climate. Humans also used their beliefs to help them make sense of their own lives—the nature of life and death and, particularly, how to escape from suffering either now or in the afterlife. They created a world of gods and goddesses and worshipped them through a system of regular rituals to ensure that the gods would look kindly upon them and the world in which they lived.

Mesopotamians

The Babylonians, like the Sumerians before them, worshipped a number of gods. They believed that Marduk, the supreme god of Babylon, created the world by building it on an enormous raft that sailed across the oceans. He also fought a huge sea monster in order to protect the world from destruction.

Egyptians

The Egyptians worshipped hundreds of different gods who they believed influenced all aspects of nature and human activity. The greatest of them all was Ra, the sun god, who created the universe. He was often shown with the head of a hawk balancing a disc on his head that produced light.

Ra—god of the sun, and creator of all living things.
Osiris—god of death and rebirth, and the ruler of the underworld.
Isis—goddess of healing and giver of life.
Sobek—the crocodile god of rivers and lakes.
Bastet—the cat goddess, protector of women.

Anubis—jackal-headed god of embalming and the dead.
Sekhmet—the lion-headed goddess of war.
Seth—god of chaos; he had the body of a man but the head of a beast known as the seth-animal.
Thoth—ibis-headed god of wisdom and writing.

Ra   Osiris   Isis   Sobek   Bastet

Anubis   Sekhmet   Seth   Thoth

SACRED OBJECTS

This early clay figure from the Stone Age is thought to be a religious idol, possibly representing the great Mother Goddess.

A ritual figure from Africa, carried by women to ensure their babies would be beautiful.

The ankh was the ancient Egyptian symbol of life. It could only be worn by pharaohs and gods, and indicates that the wearer has the power to give and take away life.

This bronze figure of a bull was left as an offering to the gods at the Greek temple at Olympia.

• Most early religions had special rituals that acted as a way of communicating with the gods. Elaborate ceremonies involved music, dance, prayers, and often the offering of money, food, or goods, or even animal or human sacrifices.

• Some things are common across most early religions, like providing answers to questions such as how the world came to be (known as creation myths), or what happens after death.

• In some religions, including those of the native peoples of North America, Australia, and Africa, the spirits of the dead were thought to live on among their ancestors. They were worshipped through objects that symbolized them, like the carved totem poles found among some Native American tribes.

This belief that spirits inhabit objects is called animism and is one of the oldest forms of religion in the world.

• In some early religions, the gods take human form. In others, such as many of the gods worshipped by the ancient Egyptians, they have human bodies but the heads of animals.

• Often the gods and goddesses of one culture would be adopted by another. The Romans, for example, worshipped many of the same gods and goddesses as those of ancient Greece—they just called them by different names.

• All over the world, our ancient ancestors built great temples and shrines in honor of their gods. Some of the most important buildings that survive today are those built for worship.

Greeks

The Greeks believed that their most important gods lived on the top of Mount Olympus in northern Greece. Their gods and goddesses all had human qualities and had symbols—often certain plants or animals—that were associated with them. The Greeks made up many stories about them —great tales of gods, monsters, and mortals that have been recorded in art and literature to this day.

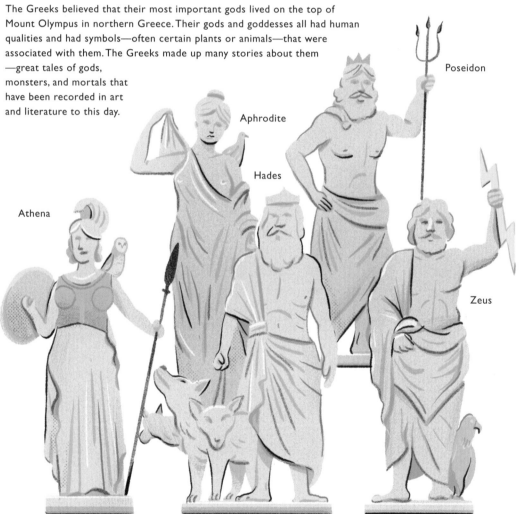

Athena

Aphrodite

Hades

Poseidon

Zeus

Mayans

The Mayans believed in an array of gods, over 250 of them, who represented aspects of nature, society, and professions. To please the maize god, Hun Hunahpu and ensure the success of their harvest, they made offerings of human blood—that of nobles was considered the best—and made human sacrifices, often taking prisoners for this very purpose.

Celts

Many of the Celtic gods were thought to live in trees, rocks, or water. Their priests, known as druids, made offerings to the gods by throwing precious objects into rivers and lakes. Sometimes they sacrificed animals or humans too.

Athena—goddess of wisdom; symbols: owl, spear, armor.
Zeus—king of the gods; symbols: oak tree, eagle, thunderbolt.
Aphrodite—goddess of love; symbols: roses, doves and dolphins.
Poseidon—god of the sea; symbols: trident, horses, dolphins.
Hades—god of the underworld; symbols: Cerberus (his three-headed dog); cornucopia (horn of plenty); cap of invisibility.

A winged sphinx, often seen guarding the entrances to palaces and temples in ancient Assyria. The Assyrians believed these monsters provided heavenly protection and warded off evil.

Japanese

The rulers of many ancient cultures were often thought to have descended directly from the gods. The ancient Japanese, for example, believed that their rulers were all descended from the Sun Goddess, Amaterasu.

MAPPING THE HEAVENS

IT IS HARDLY SURPRISING THAT FROM THE EARLIEST TIMES HUMANS HAVE BEEN FASCINATED WITH THE HEAVENS. After all, day and night—dictated by the movement of the sun—provide the basic rhythm of human existence. So it's easy to understand why primitive people were intensely interested in activity in the skies above.

Astronomy—the study of the sun, moon, stars, and space—is the oldest of the natural sciences. In early times, some cultures assembled massive monuments that are believed to have had some astronomical purpose. In addition to ceremonial uses, these megalithic observatories could help determine the change of the seasons, an important factor in knowing when to plant crops, as well

as in understanding the length of the year. For example, in some ancient structures, the stones are lined up a certain way so that the sun only rises directly behind them when it is the summer solstice (the shortest day of the year).

Astronomy was the backbone of the social, political, and religious systems of all the early civilizations, where the workings of the heavens were seen as the workings of the gods. Astronomical events had deep religious meaning for all humans and were seen as omens that could be interpreted by the powerful priest-astronomers of the time. But as civilizations developed, new ideas on the nature of the universe began to be explored, and early astronomers began to map the positions of the stars and planets.

This **Nebra sky disc** from Bronze Age Europe, made of bronze and gold, is believed to be an early instrument for making astronomical observations. It shows the sun, moon, and a number of stars— the oldest depiction of the cosmos in the world.

Below, a modern-day depiction of the **Mayan calendar**, a system of three interlacing calendars on wheels, which was used by several cultures in the ancient Americas.

EGYPT

As with most early cultures, the ancient Egyptians explained the behavior of the sky through the creation of gods. The constellation Orion, for instance, represented Osiris, the god of death, rebirth, and the afterlife. The sun itself was represented by several gods—the rising sun was Horus (the child of Osiris and Isis), the noon sun was Ra because of its incredible strength, and the evening sun became Atum, who guided the pharaohs from their tombs to the stars.

MESOPOTAMIA

The ancient Sumerians have provided us with the oldest surviving astronomical records, knowledge that has been added to and amended as it passed down through the civilizations that followed.

The Babylonian astronomers left behind them thousands of clay tablets that recorded the movement of the planets. Using this data, they developed arithmetical methods to figure out the changing length of daylight throughout the year and even to predict eclipses of the sun and moon.

INDIA

Much of what we know about ancient Indian astronomy comes from a series of sacred books called the Vedas. As in most ancient cultures, events in the heavens were believed to exert a direct effect on the people of Earth.

The earliest Veda text mentioning astronomy was written around 2000 BCE. At that time, our planet was considered to be a shell supported by elephants that were themselves standing on the back of a giant tortoise!

NEOLITHIC EUROPE

Perhaps the most mysterious form of ancient astronomy was that practiced by the Neolithic people of Western Europe, who built many giant stone structures (known as megaliths), placing them in a certain way to align with particular astronomical phenomena like sunrises or sunsets. The most famous example of this type is Stonehenge (see Chart 12), but there are many other examples around the world.

Above, a **Sumerian** clay tablet showing the constellations and fixed stars, which were believed to revolve around the Earth.

The Zodiac

The zodiac (from the Greek word meaning "circle of animals") was first developed in ancient Egypt and later adopted by the Babylonians. They identified 12 different constellations, or patterns of stars, that they believed influenced life on Earth. For example, the rainy season occurred when the sun was in the Aquarius, or water-bearer, constellation.

The **Gosek Circle**, Germany, shown here was a giant circular enclosure, erected around 4800 BCE. It is believed to have been built as a giant sun observatory—its gates align with sunrise and sunset on the summer and winter solstices (the longest and shortest days of the year).

Mayan carving of an astronomer with his eye stretched out toward the heavens.

MAYAN

The Mayans used their studies of the sky to measure the passage of time. They created a complex calendar that consisted of three interconnected calendars: a solar calendar of 365 days, a ritual calendar of 260 days—used to determine the time of religious events, and a calendar that tracked the 8,000-year long "universal cycle," at the end of which the Mayans believed the world would be destroyed and then re-created.

NATIVE AMERICAN

Many Native American tribes had complex religions of which astronomy was a large part. For example, the sun priest of the Pueblo Indians would watch for the summer solstice through a notch in the wall of a "sun tower" and, at the proper time, would announce its coming. The Pawnee, another Native American tribe, designed their lodges with astronomy in mind, laying out their villages to mirror the most important stars in the sky. Instead of the sun, they worshipped the Pleiades cluster, which contained the Pole Star, considered to be a chief protecting his people.

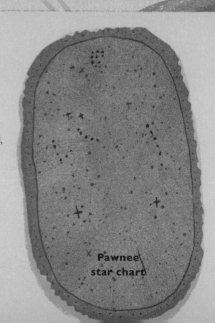

Pawnee star chart

CHINA

The ancient Chinese tended to use astronomy for practical purposes, unlike many other cultures that focused mainly on its religious aspects. Like the Mayans, one of the main purposes of Chinese astronomical observations was timekeeping. The first written records of astronomy in China are from about 3000 BCE. Over the hundreds of years of advanced sky-watching that followed, Chinese astronomers became very adept at predicting lunar eclipses and were responsible for making the first record of one in 2136 BCE.

TEMPLES AND PALACES

NOWHERE IN THE ANCIENT WORLD WAS THE SKILL of builders and craftsworkers put to more obvious use than in the temples and palaces built to honor their gods and rulers. Without any machines, some of the most enduring structures of humankind were built across the world's ancient kingdoms, the ruins of which can still be seen today.

Knossos

The palace of Knossos, above, was the ceremonial and political center of the Minoan civilization. In Greek myth, it belonged to King Minos and was home to the legendary labyrinth in which he kept his son, the Minotaur. It was supposedly so cleverly constructed that no one who entered could find their way back out without a guide. After being rebuilt several times, it was finally destroyed in 1450 BCE by a volcanic eruption.

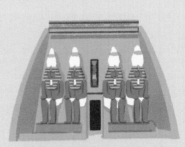

Abu Simbel
13th century BCE

The twin temples at Abu Simbel were carved out of the mountainside as a lasting monument to Rameses II and his queen Nefertari. Building lasted for about 20 years and included the carving of four colossal statues of the pharaoh, each more than 65 feet (20 meters) high. It is believed that the axis of the temple was positioned so that at certain times of year the sun would illuminate sculptures within.

Etemenanki
6th century BCE

Etemenanki (meaning "temple of the foundation of heaven and earth") is the name of a ziggurat—a type of massive stone structure with many levels—dedicated to Marduk, one of the gods of ancient Babylon. In its day, it would have towered over the ancient city, and was the focus of ceremonial processions passing through the famed Ishtar Gate. Originally 300 feet (91 meters) in height, little remains of it now.

Pyramid of the Sun
2nd century CE

The ruined Pyramid of the Sun would have dominated the landscape of Teotihuacan, the first true city of Mesoamerica in modern-day Mexico. Originally inhabited by the Toltecs and also an important Aztec site, it was most likely built to honor one of the ancient gods and likely had an altar at its top. Its base was larger than two football fields. Its surface would have originally been painted with brilliantly colored murals.

Pantheon
126 CE

This Roman temple, completed by the emperor Hadrian, was built originally to honor all gods. Its giant dome, with its famous central hole or oculus, is even now the largest unsupported dome in the world. It was made out of more than 2 million stone blocks, each weighing more than 2.5 tons. The 16 massive columns at its entrance were brought from Egypt by wooden sledge, barge and boat.

SEVEN WONDERS
OF THE ANCIENT WORLD

THE SEVEN WONDERS OF THE ANCIENT WORLD was the first known list of the most remarkable creations of classical antiquity, compiled by ancient Greek scholars over 1,000 years ago. It was based on guidebooks popular among sightseers of the time and only included works located around the Mediterranean and in Mesopotamia. The number seven was chosen because the Greeks believed it represented perfection and plenty, and because it was the number of the five planets known in those times, plus the sun and moon.

The Great Pyramid of Giza, the only wonder of the ancient world still in existence, stands on the edge of the city of Cairo in modern-day Egypt. At 481 feet (146.5 m), it was the tallest man-made structure in the world for more than 3,800 years.

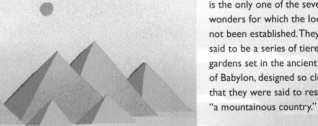

The Hanging Gardens of Babylon is the only one of the seven ancient wonders for which the location has not been established. They were said to be a series of tiered gardens set in the ancient city of Babylon, designed so cleverly that they were said to resemble "a mountainous country."

The **Lighthouse at Alexandria** at 449 feet (137 m) was once one of the tallest man-made structures in the world. It was constructed in the 3rd century BCE, took 12 years to complete and served as a prototype for all later lighthouses. The light was produced by a furnace at the top.

The **Mausoleum at Halicarnassus** was a tomb built c.350 BCE in present-day Bodrum, Turkey, for Mausolus, a governor of the Persian Empire. Destroyed by successive earthquakes, it was ranked one of the Seven Wonders of the World by the ancients because of the elegance of its design.

The Colossus of Rhodes was a statue of the Greek god of the sun, Helios, erected on the island of Rhodes in 280 BCE. It was as high as the modern Statue of Liberty in America, making it the tallest statue of the ancient world. To climb high enough to build it, workers piled huge mounds of earth on each side, which were removed at the end. Like many of the other ancient wonders, it was destroyed by earthquake.

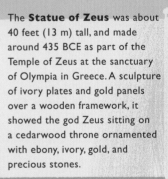

The **Statue of Zeus** was about 40 feet (13 m) tall, and made around 435 BCE as part of the Temple of Zeus at the sanctuary of Olympia in Greece. A sculpture of ivory plates and gold panels over a wooden framework, it showed the god Zeus sitting on a cedarwood throne ornamented with ebony, ivory, gold, and precious stones.

The Temple of Artemis was dedicated to the Greek goddess Artemis. It was located in Ephesus (near the modern town of Selçuk in present-day Turkey), and was completely rebuilt three times before its final destruction in 401 CE.

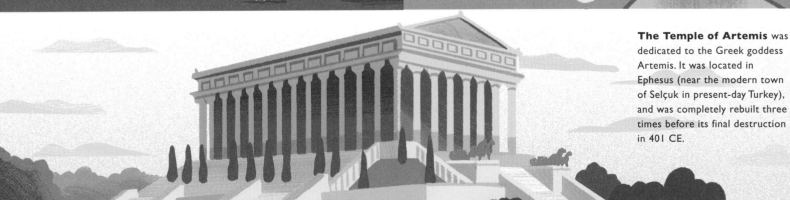

JOURNEYS OF THE DEAD

HUMAN BEINGS ARE THE ONLY CREATURES THAT BURY THEIR DEAD—a practice that goes back at least 100,000 years. The importance of a proper burial and the rituals accompanying it was emphasised by every ancient culture.
• Early pre-modern humans were probably the first to regularly bury their dead, positioning them carefully within a shallow pit and placing gifts around the body.
• In some early cultures, graves were cut deep into the earth so that the souls of the dead could more easily reach the afterlife, which was thought to exist underground.
• As human civilizations evolved, so burial ceremonies became more elaborate, especially where rulers or other important members of society were concerned.

Great tombs, like the pyramids, were created to house their bodies, often filled with amazing treasures and other objects (known as grave goods) to help them in their journey to the next world, including their guards and servants.
• Poorer people had simpler burials—often being buried below the family home so that the grave could be regularly maintained. If a person was not buried properly, it was thought that they could return as a ghost to haunt the living.
• In ancient India, most people were cremated and their ashes strewn in the waters of the River Ganges, thought to be the source of all life.

Smaller pyramids for the Pharaoh's queen and other wives

Great Pyramid of Giza

A statue of the Sphinx guards the pyramid complex

CUTAWAY OF THE MAIN PYRAMID

Airshaft
King's chamber
Grand gallery
Entrance

Tombs for the pharaohs
Ancient Egypt was ruled by pharaohs, powerful kings worshipped as gods, who are most famous for the great pyramids in which they were entombed. The Great Pyramid of Giza was built by Pharaoh Khafre to house the body of his father, Khufu, and was finished around 2560 BCE. The largest stone building ever built, it was made out of more than two million stone blocks and the base covered an area of 12 acres. The blocks were cut using simple chisels and dragged up long ramps of earth to their place in the great building.

Long Barrows, c.3500 BCE
Neolithic long barrows are among the oldest architectural structures ever built. Created as communal tombs, they were also the center of religious activity with the bones of the dead often used in ceremonies performed at the entrance to the barrow. It is thought that the barrows may have been left open so people could visit the bones of their ancestors.

Beehive tomb

Burial inside tomb

Gold death mask

Beehive burials, c.1500 BCE
In Mycenea, kings were buried with their belongings in huge, beehive-shaped tombs built under great mounds of earth. Earlier, kings had been buried with their families in deep pits, called shaft graves. Hard to rob, much of the treasure with which they were buried has survived, such as this gold mask.

A model army
The tradition of being buried with your most precious possessions was taken to an extreme by the first emperor of China, Qin Shi Huang. When he died in 210 BCE he was buried in a huge tomb guarded by a replica of his army—over 7,500 life-size warriors made out of terra-cotta. They carried real crossbows that were said to be set to fire automatically at anyone who tried to break into the tomb.

HOW TO MAKE A MUMMY

THE ANCIENT EGYPTIANS BELIEVED THAT IF YOUR BODY ROTTED OR WAS DAMAGED IN DEATH, it would spoil your chances of having a happy afterlife. So rather than simply burying or burning dead bodies, the Egyptians developed a technique to preserve them—a form of embalming known as mummification. Only the rich could afford to be mummified—the poor were simply buried in the sands of the desert.

1 First the body was washed in wine. Then a priest (often wearing the jackal mask of Anubis, god of the dead) would remove the internal organs (except for the heart, which was believed to be the home of the person's spirit). Special hooks were used to pull the brain out through the nostrils!

2 The body cavity was then filled with a special substance called natron (a natural salt) and left for 40 days to dry out.

3 After being stuffed with sawdust, the body was rubbed with perfumed oils, coated with resin, and then wrapped in layers of linen bandage. Amulets (pieces of jewelry with magical powers) were often put among the wrappings to keep the spirit safe on its journey to the afterlife.

4 The mummy was placed in a special coffin, called a sarcophagus, often painted or carved with a likeness of the dead person inside. The mummy's face was often covered separately with a decorated mask. The mummies of important people were often enclosed in several coffins, with the inner one sometimes being made of gold or silver, which sat inside large wooden shrines.

Outer sarcophagus of painted wood

5 The mummy was finally laid to rest exactly 70 days after death. A funeral procession would carry the coffin and burial goods to the tomb, where they would be sealed in so robbers could not enter and steal things.

A

B
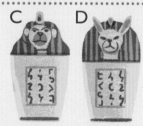
C   D

CANOPIC JARS

Once removed, a person's internal organs were stored in special containers known as canopic jars. Each jar was decorated with one of four different heads, representing the four sons of Horus, god of the sky.
A. **Imsety** had a human head and protected the liver.
B. **Qebhsenuf** had the head of a falcon and guarded the intestines.
C. **Hapy** had a baboon head and protected the lungs.
D. **Duamatef** had the head of a jackal, and guarded the stomach.
Once the mummification process was complete, the jars would be stored in a special chest which went into the tomb with the mummy.

WEIGHING THE HEART

The Egyptians believed that when a person died, their spirit undertook a perilous journey to the afterworld. Each person's heart would be weighed against the feather of truth by Anubis to measure their worth. Good people would pass through to a happy afterlife but those found wanting were devoured by Ammit—a beast with the head of a crocodile, the body of a lion, and the rear of a hippopotamus.

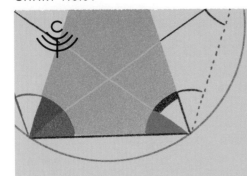

BREAKTHROUGHS IN

HUMANS HAVE ALWAYS TRIED TO MAKE SENSE OF THE WORLD AROUND THEM, INVENTING EXPLANATIONS FOR NATURAL PHENOMENA AND STUDYING THEIR ENVIRONMENT IN AN ATTEMPT TO SOLVE ITS MYSTERIES. With the coming of the first great civilizations, humans realized that with careful thinking and observation, it was possible to find patterns in the workings of the natural world, and that those patterns were the key to unlocking the secrets of the universe. By knowing those patterns, or rules, one could learn to predict the behavior of nature.

In many early cultures, although humans learned to accurately make such predictions, their explanations for why and how things happened was often put down to the work of gods or other supernatural beings. It was the great thinkers of ancient Greece who began to replace the idea of a world ruled by gods with a universe governed by the laws of nature. They tried to develop theories behind their observations and, together, they made some of the biggest breakthroughs in understanding the nature of the world. Although some of their ideas were later proved wrong, many of their discoveries and inventions are still in use today and their achievements helped shape the foundations of Western civilization.

THE BIRTH OF SCIENCE

Science—the knowledge of natural processes—has existed since the dawn of human existence, but understanding why and how these processes took place were mysteries that took thousands of years to solve.

• The English word "scientist" did not come into use until the 19th century. The ancient Greeks, who set themselves the task of understanding more about the world 2,500 years ago, called themselves "natural philosophers," and it was out of their studies that the modern branches of physics, chemistry, and biology sprung.

• **Thales of Miletus**, known as the "Father of Science," was one of the first Greek scholars to proclaim that every event had a natural cause rather than being the work of the gods.

• **Aristotle**, the father of zoology, studied plants, animals, and rocks, categorizing over 500 different species. He laid the foundations for modern science with his belief in the rationality and orderliness of the world. He also believed that all matter was made up of a combination of four elements: earth, water, air, and fire—a belief that lasted until the 15th century!

• **Aristarchus** was the first person to propose that the sun was at the center of the universe and that Earth and all the other planets revolved around it, an idea so ahead of its time that it was originally disregarded as blasphemy.

• **Eudoxus** made a map of the known stars, and used mathematics to explain astronomical phenomena, turning astronomy into a science.

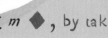

THE WISDOM OF PHILOSOPHERS

Western philosophy, which means "love of wisdom," began in ancient Greece around the 6th century BCE. The early philosophers asked important questions about the nature of existence, being, and the world (known as metaphysics).

Philosophy really took off, though, with **Socrates** in the 5th century BCE. Socrates was concerned with how people should behave, and was perhaps the first major philosopher of ethics. He developed a system to work out how to live properly and to tell the difference between right and wrong. His student **Plato**—perhaps the best known, most widely studied, and most influential philosopher of all time—believed that virtue was a kind of knowledge (the knowledge of good and evil) that all humans needed in order to reach their full potential.

The third in the main trio of classical philosophers was Plato's student **Aristotle**. He created an even more comprehensive system of philosophy than Plato—which included the belief that knowledge should come from study, analysis, experience, and reason—and his work influenced almost all later philosophical thinking.

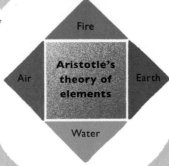

Aristotle's theory of elements

Fire

Air

Earth

Water

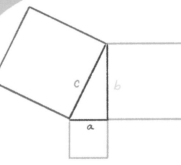

Euclidian geometry deals with points, lines, and planes, and how they interact to make complex figures.

Pythagoras' Theorem states that for all right-angled triangles: "the square on the hypotenuse (the side opposite the right angle) is equal to the sum of the squares on the other two sides." This famous formula can be used to test whether a triangle has a right angle or not and therefore to formulate perfect rectangles and squares. It was, and continues to be, of enormous use to builders.

THINKING

MARVELOUS MEDICINE

The people of the ancient world did not do too well when it came to curing diseases. In many cultures, illness was thought of as a punishment doled out by the gods, and all possible remedies were surrounded by superstition. That all changed when **Hippocrates**, an ancient Greek physician, started to study illness, collecting data and conducting experiments to show that disease was a natural process. He believed that the signs and symptoms of disease were caused by the natural reactions of the body and that doctors should observe symptoms in order to determine how to treat a patient. Often referred to as the Father of Western Medicine, he wrote over

50 books on the subject and was the originator of the Hippocratic Oath, a text that established several principles of medical ethics that are still followed by doctors today, including the commitment to "do no harm."

The **Rod of Asclepius** is a serpent-entwined rod wielded by Asclepius, the Greek god of healing and medicine. The symbol is still used today, and is associated with medicine and health care.

MATHEMATICS

Marks made on bones from prehistoric times indicate that early humans were recording numbers long before the advent of writing. When civilizations started to flourish, humans needed more complex forms of counting to help them make financial calculations for trade and taxes, measure land, record time, and construct increasingly impressive buildings. The ancient Greeks, inspired by the Egyptians and Babylonians, developed an understanding of mathematics that was much more sophisticated than that of earlier cultures.

• **Pythagoras** established the Pythagorean School, whose doctrine was that mathematics ruled the universe and whose motto was "All is number." It was the Pythagoreans who coined the term "mathematics."

• **Archimedes**, considered one of the greatest mathematicians of all time, made many scientific discoveries. He discovered that submerging a solid object will displace an amount of liquid that matches the object's weight (known as Archimedes' principle) and developed various other mathematical rules that would influence later scholars.

• **Euclid**, the "Father of Geometry," wrote the *Elements*, widely considered the most influential mathematical textbook of all time. Its contents are still taught today.

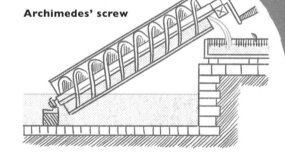

Archimedes' screw

Archimedes invented the screw that bears his name—a mechanism that could be used to raise water for irrigation. When turned, the screw collected water at the bottom, which was then forced upward and out of the top by the turning motion of the screw.

Archimedes' principle

ALL THE WORLD'S A STAGE…

HUMANS HAVE ALWAYS LOVED TO BE ENTERTAINED. Even early humans would gather around a fire, to dance, sing, play music, and while away the hours of darkness by telling tales passed down from their ancestors.

Storytelling, music, drama, and dance existed in all ancient cultures and became more sophisticated as human societies became more complex. Some of these entertainments were invented as individual pursuits designed to help pass the time; others could be used to entertain thousands of spectators and were an important way in which rulers attempted to keep their subjects happy. Some entertainments went beyond simple gratification to convey important messages to their audience—about the meaning of life, the importance of obedience, or, in the case of the ancient Greeks, to address universal philosophical questions such as "What does it mean to be human?"

In medieval times, people known as troubadours traveled from one village to the next singing songs that told stories of courtly love and the latest news, as well as tales from far-off lands and historical events. They were often found in traveling bands including other performers, such as musicians, conjurers, acrobats, jesters, and jugglers.

THE POWER OF STORIES

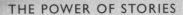

The ancient craft of telling stories has been an important part of most forms of entertainment since the earliest times. As they couldn't write things down, storytelling was the means by which the ancients passed on their traditions and history from one generation to another. It was a way for people to express their fears and their beliefs, and try to explain the world. In fact, the art of telling stories has probably been around as long as human language has existed.

As societies evolved, the ability to tell stories emerged as a valuable skill. Stories began to emerge as a way to preserve our history as well as a form of entertainment—a way of chronicling the story of our past.
• Early storytelling often combined stories, poetry, music, and dance, and evolved into other forms, such as theater, where stories were bought to life in different ways.

• The earliest evidence of storytelling comes from the Lascaux caves in southern France. Here, a series of paintings dating back to around 13,000 BCE depict a variety of animals and one image of a human being. When closely examined, these images depict a simple series of events: rituals and a hunt. They tell a story.
• The first recorded story, the *Epic of Gilgamesh*, was created in Mesopotamia around 2,000 BCE.

It tells the tale of the historical King of Uruk and was originally written on 12 clay tablets in cuneiform.
• In ancient Greece, a slave called Aesop created a series of fables that are still told to children today,.
• Medieval storytellers were expected to know popular tales as well as general news and gossip. They could often be found in marketplaces telling their tales and were honored as members of royal courts.

The history of board games goes back to the earliest civilizations. In ancient Egypt, two of the most popular board games were senet and mehen. Mehen was played on a round board with spaces shaped like a coiled snake. Senet, which represented the journey of the dead into the afterlife, was so popular that many pharaohs were buried with senet boards.

TIME TO DANCE

No one knows who invented dancing, but it would seem to be a very natural form of human expression. The very first records of dancing are found in India and Egypt c.3300 BCE, but dancing as a means of expression or entertainment, as part of a religious ritual or celebration, or as part of storytelling has probably existed for hundreds of thousands of years.

• In many cultures, dance was an important part of rituals. Most classical dances of India tell stories from Hindu mythology. The Hindu god Shiva is also known by the name Nataraja, lord of a dance in which the world is both created and destroyed.

• In Africa, dance occupied a central place in many cultures throughout the continent, where ritual dance was seen as a way of communicating with the gods.

This dancer is performing the Bharatanatyam, which combines the four most important aspects of Indian classical dance: emotion, melody, rhythm, and meaning.

Stilt walking was a popular form of entertainment in ancient China. Dancers would strap long pieces of bamboo to their feet and perform folk dances for the entertainment of the emperor.

ANCIENT ACTORS

The first great plays in the world were written by the ancient Greeks, who used drama as a way of questioning the nature of the world. Two thousand years later, one of the greatest playwrights of all, William Shakespeare, would write plays that were often inspired by stories from the ancient world.

• Ancient Greek plays were part of religious festivals and the Greeks built great amphitheaters in which to stage them. The cast comprised of amateurs rather than professionals, and all the actors were male.

• The three genres of Greek drama were comedy, satyr plays, and, most important of all, tragedy. The great philosopher and playwright Aristotle said that tragedy cleansed the heart and made us forget our everyday worries.

• In Southeast Asia, shadow theater is an ancient form of entertainment that uses cutout figures (shadow puppets) instead of real people to act out stories for an audience.

In ancient Greece, actors wore exaggerated masks to show what characters they were playing. Tragic masks carried mournful or pained expressions, while comic masks were smiling or leering.

Chinese shadow puppets

SPECTATOR SPORTS

Many kinds of sport are seen as a form of entertainment, but the Romans took spectator sport to new heights, building stadiums in which thousands of people could be entertained—though by today's standards, the sport they watched was both bloody and brutal.

• The Circus Maximus was the first and largest stadium in ancient Rome and could accommodate over 150,000 spectators who came to watch ludi—public games connected to religious festivals. Some events lasted for several days and involved religious ceremonies, public feasts, chariot racing, athletics, plays and recitals, beast-hunts, and gladiator fights.

• Gladiatorial combats were a combination of sport, punishment, and entertainment. The most famous venue for these was Rome's Colosseum, the world's largest amphitheater. As well as gladiatorial contests, in which slaves would fight each other, often to the death, it was used to stage macabre public spectacles, such as, animal hunts, executions, and reenactments of famous battles.

3

THE WORLD IN TUNE

ALONG WITH DANCE, MUSIC IS ONE OF THE VERY OLDEST ART FORMS. It has been an essential part of all human cultures for nearly 50,000 years.

It is likely that the first musical instrument was the human voice itself, an instrument used to make all sorts of sounds in the name of music—from singing to humming, clicking to whistling—since those early times. Then came the need for percussion—first hands and feet, then sticks, rocks, and logs as our music-making evolved to include rhythm and beat.

The development of materials allowed us to make an array of new, different noises—clay rattles, pottery horns, and, with the discovery of metals, a host of bells, chimes, cymbals, and gongs. Most of these early musical objects could make only a single noise or note, but soon simple flutes, hollowed from bone or wood, which could play more than one note became common in many cultures. The addition of reeds (which vibrate to produce a sound) to the mouthpiece of wind instruments was an invention of the ancient Egyptians, the forerunner of today's oboes, clarinets, and bassoons.

Musical instruments developed independently in many regions of the world, but as trade increased, contact among civilizations caused the rapid spread and adaptation of most instruments in places far from their origin.

A Chinese xiqin from the Tang dynasty

For thousands of years, music was passed on by listening and repetition. No accurate system of writing it down existed until monks in the 9th century first used musical notation. But from the remains of ancient instruments and the art and descriptions of them left behind, we have an idea of the music that filled the air in those ancient days.

• Many early musical instruments were developed for a practical purpose. Some started as a means of communication—drums were used to relay messages across long distances, horns as signals during a hunt, and both played a crucial role in battles.

• Musical instruments also had important religious, spiritual, and ceremonial applications and were an integral part of the ritual behavior of humans the world over.

• Early instruments were often made from "found objects" such as shells or bones. The oldest musical instrument discovered so far is a flute made from the femur of a bear, thought to be 40,000 years old.

• During the Renaissance period, instruments were used as solo instruments rather than simply providing the accompaniment to singing or dancing. Keyboards and lutes developed as polyphonic instruments (capable of producing more than one note at a time), and composers arranged increasingly complex musical compositions that required many instruments to play together in the first orchestras.

PERCUSSIVE

KEY TO ILLUSTRATION

A. **Aztec ayotl**—empty tortoise shells were rubbed with a notched stick to produce sound and were used along with other percussion instruments to accompany ritual dances. Human skulls were also used in the same way!

B. **Wooden fish**—a hollow vessel, struck to provide the rhythm during Buddhist religious chants. The very first examples were actually fish-shaped.

C. **Zeng bell**—an ancient Chinese musical instrument consisting of

many bronze bells like this, each capable of playing two notes.

D. **Indian frame drum**—reputed to be the first type of drum ever invented.

E. **Egyptian sistrum** (rattle)—percussion instrument common in many cultures. Made from clay, wood, or metal, it provided rhythmical accompaniment to other instruments, particularly in religious rites and festivals.

F. **African djembe**—dating from the 1st century CE, these

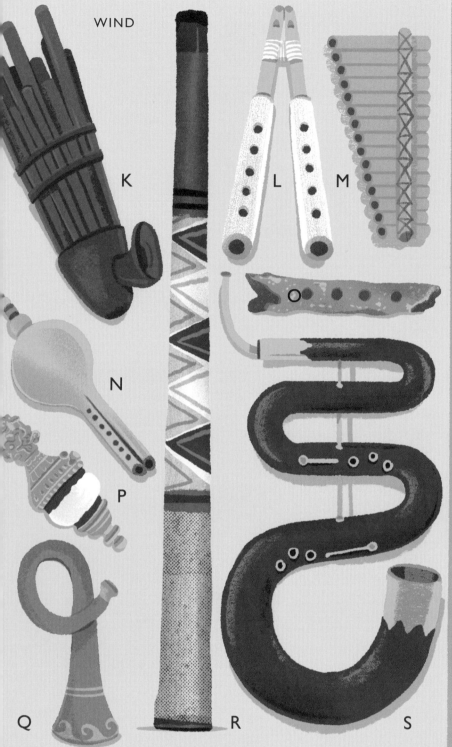

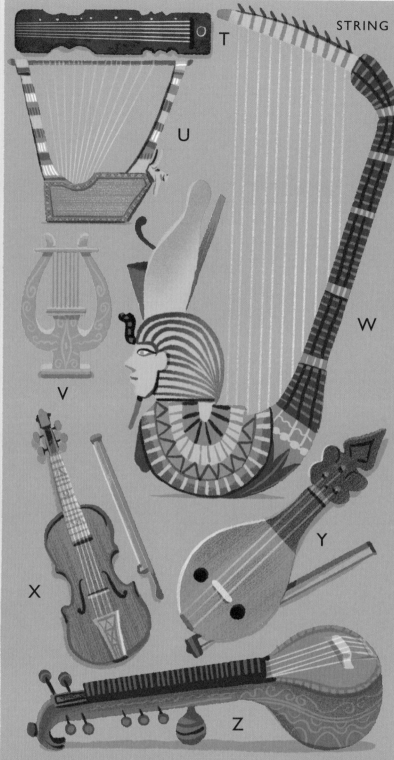

K

L

M

N

O

P

Q

R

S

T

U

V

W

X

Y

Z

42

skin-covered goblet drums can make a variety of sounds and are tuned using the rope bindings.

G. Viking drum beater

H. Wooden slit drum—slit drums are not "true" drums but ancient instruments made from hollow lengths of wood or bamboo. When you hit the top, they vibrate to make a sound.

I. Bullroarer—a ritual instrument dating to the Paleolithic period that makes a roaring sound when spun in a circle. It was also used for communicating over extended distances.

J. Xylophone—the earliest xylophones—made of individual bars of wood that could be used to play a musical scale—were known in both Southeast Asia and Africa around 500 CE.

K. Sheng—a Chinese reed instrument from 1100 BCE.

L. Aulos—a reeded double flute from ancient Greece.

M. Panpipes—commonly played by shepherds in ancient Greece.

N. Indian pungi—made from a dried type of fruit called a bottle gourd, these instruments were used to charm snakes.

O Neanderthal bone flute

P. Shankha—a shell trumpet, sacred emblem of the Hindu god Vishnu, which is still used in Hindu ritual and, in the past, as a war trumpet.

Q. Clay trumpet—the Moche people of ancient Peru depicted trumpets in their art going back to 300 CE.

R. Didgeridoo—made of eucalyptus wood hollowed out by termites, this ancient aboriginal instrument has been played for tens of thousands of years.

S. Serpent—first seen during the Renaissance, this is the distant ancestor of the tuba.

T. Guqin—the earliest known surviving instrument of the zither family is a Chinese guqin, found in the tomb of Marquis Yi of Zeng dating from 433 BCE.

U. Lyre of Ur—at over 4,500 years old, the lyres found in the Sumerian city of Ur are the world's oldest surviving stringed instruments.

V. Greek lyre—transformed into an S-shape, the Greek lyre was one of the symbols of Hermes, the messenger god.

W Egyptian harps were often depicted in tomb paintings.

X. Violin—the modern four-string violin is generally considered to have originated about 1550 in northern Italy.

Y. Lyra—the Byzantine lyra is the ancestor of most European bowed instruments, including the violin.

Z. Indian veena—the ancestor of today's hollow stringed instruments, the veena first appeared c.600 BCE.

THE SPORTING LIFE

SINCE ANCIENT TIMES PEOPLE HAVE PLAYED SPORTS—whether for sheer personal pleasure, the joy of playing as part of a team, or as part of a religious ritual. Many of today's sports have their origins in long-ago times, often evolving from activities that originally had a more serious intent—as part of the hunt for food or to increase success in battle.

• Cave paintings have been found in the Lascaux caves in France that may depict humans sprinting and wrestling around 15,300 years ago.

• In many early cultures, sporting pursuits reflected the needs of military training—archery, boxing, charioteering, horsemanship, wrestling—with competition used as a means to determine whether individuals were fit and useful for service.

• In most cultures, women rarely participated in sports of any kind. In ancient Greece, they were excluded from the Olympic Games, even as spectators.

• The sports of medieval Europe were less well organized. At fairs and festivals, men lifted stones or sacks of grain and women ran smock races (for a smock, not in one!). The favorite sport of the peasantry was soccer.

Boxing and wrestling

Various representations of wrestlers have been found on stone slabs recovered from the Sumerian civilization. Dating from around 3000 BCE, they are some of the earliest depictions of sports.

The ancient Greeks believed fist fighting was one of the games played by the gods. During Roman times, boxers fought with leather bands around their fists, sometimes covered in metal studs, resulting in bloody battles. Often slaves were made to fight in a circle marked on the floor, the origin of the term "ring."

Sumo

Martial arts similar to sumo have been performed around the world since long ago. In Japan, figurines of sumo wrestlers have been unearthed dating back to the 7th century CE. When it was time to plant the yearly rice crop, sumo competitions were performed as a way to pray for a bountiful crop. Many aspects of old Japan remain in sumo today, such as topknots, traditional dress, and ancient customs.

Gladiators

Gladiators originally performed at funerals, fighting to the death with the intent of providing the deceased with armed attendants in the next world. As a spectator sport, gladiatorial contests were wildly popular in ancient Rome, with as many as 300 pairs performing in a single competition.

THE OLYMPICS

Boxing

Long jump

Arguably the most famous sporting competiton of the ancient world, the Olympic Games were first perfomed in Olympia in 776 BCE. In Greece, sport had a cultural significance unequaled anywhere else. Originally a religious festival in honor of the god Zeus, the games were held every four years, or Olympiad, which became a unit of time in historical chronologies. Initially a single sprinting event, the Olympics gradually expanded to include several foot races (run in the nude or in armor), boxing, wrestling, pankration (a form of hand-to-hand fighting), chariot racing, long jump, javelin, and discus. During the celebration of the games, an Olympic Truce was enacted so that in times of war athletes could travel from their countries to the games in safety. The prizes for the victors were wreaths of laurel leaves.

Mayan ball game

The Mayan ball game of pitz, similar to racketball, is believed to be the first ball sport, originally played around 2500 BCE. It had different rules in different places and a newer, more modern version of the game, ulama, is still played in South America today. Games were played between two teams of players on stone ballcourts, and involved throwing a solid rubber ball, sometimes weighing as much as 9 pounds (4 kg), through vertical stone rings on each side of the court using only the hips. This ancient hip ball was made from various latex-producing plants found in the region. The game could be brutal and there were often serious injuries inflicted by the solid, heavy ball.

Running

Javelin

Discus

Wrestling

Chariot racing

The origins of soccer

Ball games have been played for millennia all over the world, using everything from carefully sewn and stuffed skins or animal bladders to gourds (a kind of plant), chunks of wood, or rounded stones. But the origins of one of today's most popular ball sports, soccer, had its beginnings in Han-dynasty China. Descriptions of the game cuju (which literally means "kicking ball") have been found in a military manual dating back to this period. Players had to use their feet, chest, back, and shoulders to aim a leather ball filled with feathers and hair at a target while withstanding the attacks of their opponents. Use of the hands was not permitted.

Persian polo

Evolving from a game played by the nomads of Central Asia in which hundreds of mounted tribesmen fought over the head from a carcass of a goat, polo was a training game for Persian cavalry units. In time, it became a national sport played extensively by the nobility.

Bull leaping

Ritual sporting events are seen in the Minoan art of Bronze Age Crete, with frescoes showing various forms of gymnastics, including the art of bull-leaping. It is uncertain whether the spectacle was simply a test of acrobatic skills, part of a religious ritual, or both.

Chariot racing was one of the most popular sports in ancient Greece, Rome, and Byzantium. A dangerous pursuit for both drivers and horses, as many as 150,000 spectators would flock to the races held in Rome's Circus Maximus—five times the number that crowded into the Colosseum to enjoy gladiatorial combat.

Jousting tournaments were a favorite sport of medieval knights. At the tilt, in which mounted knights tried to unhorse one another, they were in effect practicing the art of war, displaying their skills, and profiting not only from valuable prizes but also from ransoms exacted from the losers.

ANIMALS AND HUMANS

OUR RELATIONSHIP WITH THE ANIMALS THAT SHARE OUR PLANET HAS BEEN AN ESSENTIAL PART OF THE HUMAN STORY. They have provided us with food, transportation, clothing, and companionship; we have both used and abused them, made them objects of worship and revered them as symbols of status. The study of animals has helped us increase our knowledge of the world, from understanding the evolution of life to the inner workings of our own bodies. Whether by taming individual wild creatures to do our bidding, or breeding new types of animal through centuries of domestication, we have used them in myriad ways to further our own successful evolution.

• Humans have collected animals both for study and entertainment since ancient times. One of the earliest menageries dates from ancient Egypt and included hippopotami,

KEY TO ILLUSTRATION

A. It is not known when the first beehive was developed, but by the time of the ancient Greeks, **bees** were being kept in woven domes, known as a skeps. As well as providing honey and beeswax, both the Greeks and Romans also used bees as tiny weapons of war, catapulting beehives over the walls of cities under siege.

B. The **dog** was the first animal species to be domesticated, way back when our ancestors were still living as hunter-gatherers. Over the many thousands of years that followed, we bred dogs for any number of uses, from hunting to herding, pulling loads and providing protection, or, more recently, simply as pets. It was a dog's incredible sense of smell and the way this could be used to help humans hunt for food that was probably its most useful attribute. Without dogs to help us, we humans would

have found our evolutionary journey much harder.

C. **Cats** were first domesticated in Egypt some 15,000 years ago, where they were regarded as sacred animals, mummified in their millions to be buried in tombs alongside their owners. The cat has often been portrayed as a creature of mystery and magic, the natural companion for witches, but despite this reputation, the ownership of cats had a much more practical purpose, for they have long

been revered as excellent killers of vermin. Farmers of all nations have used cats to keep their grain stores free of mice and their use on ships helped keep the rats away from the crew's supply of food. In fact, it was their role as ship's cat, beloved of all ancient mariners, that helped spread the domestic cat around the world.

D. Although less popular now, **rabbits** have been bred as a source of food and fur since Roman times. Thanks to the speed with which they breed,

they were often introduced on to islands to establish a living larder for passing ships.

E. Humans acquired another of their most important animal allies when they domesticated the **horse** in about 3000 BCE. Originally hunted as a source of meat, the use of horses as a means of transportation rapidly spread throughout the world. Horses have also played an important part in warfare since ancient times. The invention of the saddle and stirrup, along with the breeding

elephants, hartebeest, baboons, and wildcats.

• All domesticated breeds of animal—from the many different sizes and shapes of horse, dog, cat, chicken, sheep— are the result of selective breeding by humans, often from a single wild species. By choosing to breed only from individual creatures that displayed particular characteristics—a good yield of meat or wool, or a gentle temperament, for example—we have bred animals to be of the greatest use to mankind.

• The first animals known to have been domesticated as a source of food were sheep and goats, followed by cattle and pigs. In addition to meat and milk, these animals also provided early humans with manure for their crops, leather and wool for their clothing, horn and bone for needles and arrows, fat and oil for candles, and hooves for glue.

• Many creatures have been put to use by man as beasts of burden, made to pull or carry loads, or as mounts for us to ride. Horses, donkeys, mules, camels, oxen, elephants, yaks, and reindeer have all been used in this way.

• Animals were not commonly kept as pets until medieval times and even then this was only seen in wealthy households. Near the end of this period the word "pet" (from "petty" meaning small) was introduced into the English language.

of larger types of horses that could carry a rider in heavy armor, heralded the arrival of battles involving mounted warriors c.500 BCE. Horses and mounted cavalry have played a part in almost every major war since those times.
F. Animals have long been used to provide entertainment, from the horse races of the ancient Greeks to the barbaric beast fights of the Roman circus. **Dancing bears** were commonplace throughout Europe and Asia

from the Middle Ages to the 19th century, often found accompanying musicians and a familiar sight at traveling fairs.
G. Pigeons were first kept by the ancient Egyptians as a reliable source of protein, but they have been used to carry messages since at least the 6th century BCE, when the Persian king Cyrus is said to have used pigeons to communicate with the distant parts of his empire.
H. The art of **falconry**, using a trained bird of prey to hunt for wild game, most likely

began some 4,000 years ago. By the medieval period, it was a popular sport among the nobles of Europe, the Middle East, and the Mongol Empire.
I. Humans have enlisted animals to help them fight their wars since prehistoric times. Dogs and horses were probably the first animals used in war, but **elephants** also made their mark. Capable of creating devastation among packed formations of enemy troops, they were often heavily armored for battle

with their tusks tipped with iron spikes. Elephants were first used in war in India around the 4th century BCE and their use spread through Persia to Greece and then to Rome. Ultimately, they proved unsuited to war, being too likely to panic and often causing as much damage to their own forces as they did to those of their enemies.
J. For thousands of years, fishermen have used trained **cormorants** to fish the rivers and lakes of China. The birds

are controlled using a snare tied near the base of the bird's throat to prevent it swallowing its catch. This traditional fishing method has been used in both Japan and China since about the 1st century CE and is still practiced today.
K. The use of **pigs** to hunt truffles, a type of fungus highly prized among chefs, is said to date back to the Roman Empire, when truffle hogs were trained to locate and root them out from as deep as 3 feet (1m) underground.

ROMAN ROADS

Few vehicles are much use without a system of trails on which to use them. The first "roads" were simply earth tracks created by the foot traffic of humans, but from 300 BCE, the Romans created a lasting legacy of road networks, many of which survive today. Eventually over 250,000 miles (400,000 kilometers) of their stone-paved roads stretched from Scotland through Eastern Europe to Mesopotamia and North Africa. The system was so well set up that commanders could accurately calculate how long it would take their armies to march from one place to another. Being able to move troops and supplies around with greater ease was a crucial factor in the success of the Roman Empire.

Roman soldiers on the Appian Way

ACROSS THE LAND

HUMANS HAVE NEEDED TO MOVE FROM ONE PLACE TO ANOTHER SINCE THE EARLIEST TIMES, to find food, explore new territories, or to trade goods with their neighbors. For centuries, the only way to move around on land was to walk, and to carry goods we had to rely on our own brute strength.

As human society evolved, we invented means that allowed us to travel farther and faster (and in greater comfort) than ever before. Firstly, we tamed animals to carry things for us. Then the invention of the wheel around 3500 BCE, and the development of wheeled transportation that followed, revolutionized both our ability to get around and the load that could be transported in one go. Even so, up until the inventions of the 1800s and the arrival of mechanical engines, our available means of getting around over land were severely limited. For thousands of years, it could take us days to travel even a few miles, and years to make journeys that we can now complete in a single day.

• Walking was the first form of transport and the most widely used until only 200 years ago, so one very important aid to travel came in the form of foot coverings—from the earliest leather shoes of the prehistoric era to a Roman soldier's sandals, complete with hobnails in the soles for durability.

• Similarly, the invention of skis and snowshoes had an enormous impact on our ability to travel on ground covered in heavy snow or ice and were first used by humans many thousands of years ago. Rock paintings and physical remains found preserved in bogs show that hunters used skis at least 5,000 years ago, as they followed reindeer and elk herds across the frozen lands of the Far North.

• Sleds were another early form of transportation commonly used to move goods, pulled either by humans or animals. They were useful for transporting goods not just over snow but over many forms of rough or soft ground where wheels would have encountered difficulties. The first animals used to pull sleds were probably oxen, though mules, horses, and dogs were also used.

• Pack animals have been used to carry goods since Neolithic times. Loaded up with side bags, known as panniers, they could carry very heavy loads across difficult terrain and continue to be used in many parts of the world even today.

• Around 5,000 years ago, the wheel—first used in the making of pottery—was adapted as a means of transport. Early wheels were carved from stone before lighter wooden wheels were invented.

Viking skier

Pack mule and load

Nomadic herder on horseback

Prehistoric cart showing a solid wooden wheel

Dog sled

BRIDGES

Early bridges were simple structures built from easily accessible natural resources, such as tree trunks or logs. Because of that, they could only span short distances and were highly unstable, often being washed away in storms and bad weather.

A revolution in bridge construction came with the ancient Romans. Their bridges were built with stone and had arches as part of their basic design. Most importantly they used concrete, which the Romans invented, to hold the stones in place. Roman bridges could span greater distances than any bridge before them

and were so strong that many survive today. In the Americas the Incas created a quite different form of bridge—the rope suspension bridge—to help them travel quickly across the deep canyons and steep river valleys of their mountainous empire. The bridges were built using natural fibers woven together to create strong rope

and reinforced with wood slats to create walkways. The ropes were attached to a pair of stone anchors on either side of the crossing. The Inca people had no wheeled transport so traffic was limited to pedestrians and livestock, often including runners delivering messages across the Inca Empire.

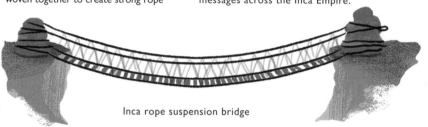

Roman many-arched stone bridge

Inca rope suspension bridge

At first, they were made of solid pieces of wood lashed together to form a circle, but after 2000 BCE, they were made with spokes.

• Animals were used to pull wheeled vehicles long before they were ridden as a form of transportation. A carving from the Sumerian city of Ur, dated to 2500 BCE, shows a king being carried in one of the world's first wheeled vehicles, pulled by four onagers (donkey-like animals).

• Another early form of transport for rich or important people was to be carried in a litter like the palanquin shown below—in its most simple form, a chair was suspended between two poles, although some were as big as beds, complete with pillows. Many types of litter have existed all over the world since ancient times.

• Humans have ridden animals for transportation for thousands of years, from mules to camels, and even elephants. But the adoption of horses for riding was one of the most important steps in the story of our ability to travel long distances with relative ease. Horses are believed to have been domesticated from wild horses in Central Asia about 6,000 years ago and their use spread rapidly as a means of transport, as beasts of burden, for hunting and warfare, as well as just for the pleasure of riding.

• Compared to land travel, journeys by some kind of boat were quicker, easier, and often far more comfortable. You can find out more about the history of boats on pages 70–71.

WHEELED VEHICLES

Early wheeled vehicles were simple wagons or sleds with a wheel attached to each side. They were generally used to transport goods rather than people and could be pulled by hand as well as by a variety of animals. Over time, more sophisticated forms of wheeled vehicles appeared—open chariots for hunting and warfare, covered carriages that allowed for more comfortable journeys, and coaches that could carry many people.

• The earliest recorded type of carriage was the chariot, seen in Mesopotamia as early as 1900 BCE, first used for hunting but later adapted for warfare. An ancient Egyptian chariot, pulled by a pair of horses, could reach speeds of up to 18 mph with ease.

• One of the great innovations in carriage design was the invention of suspension, probably by the Romans, where the traveling compartment swung on chains or leather straps attached to the wheeled frame. This formed the basis of all suspension systems until the 19th century

and made for a much less bumpy ride.

• In the 1400s, the Hungarians developed a fast-moving carriage to travel between Budapest and Vienna, stopping at the post town of Kocs (pronounced "kotch") along the way. So the "coach" was born, and its use soon spread throughout Europe.

• The wheelbarrow, invented in Han China, was a single-wheeled vehicle that revolutionized the lives of farmers who could push their heavy loads in barrows instead of having to carry them. The earliest wheelbarrows were used around 200 BCE by soldiers in the Chinese army, to transport their supplies along narrow embankments. They were later also used to carry people.

• By the end of the medieval period, the roads were home to all kinds of carts, wagons, and carriages. Those owned by the rich were often elaborately furnished inside and out, with gilded woodwork and palatial interiors. The heavier the furnishings however, the slower the progress!

Egyptian war chariot

Indian palanquin

Medieval gilded carriage

A BRIEF HISTORY OF BOATS

WITHOUT THE INVENTION OF BOATS, HUMANS WOULD NOT HAVE BEEN ABLE TO COLONIZE MANY PARTS OF THE WORLD. They are the means by which we could move beyond the boundaries of the great landmasses and set forth across the world's oceans to find new lands. Boats were essential from early times in expanding the horizons of individual communities and culture, providing the means for us to trade with other lands, swapping not just goods but ideas, inventions, and beliefs. They were also important instruments of war.

The oldest recovered boat in the world is a dugout made from the hollowed trunk of a pine tree and constructed somewhere between 8200 and 7600 BCE. Other early boats were probably nothing more than bundles of logs or reeds, lashed together with vines. Once the principle of a watertight hull was understood, the primitive boat-builder was already on their way toward the only design of wooden boat capable of being built on a large scale—a frame to which a keel (a structural beam acting as a backbone) could be attached. This principle links the simple river boats of the ancient Egyptians to the many-masted galleons of the 16th century.

Prehistory

Simple log rafts were probably the first boats made by humans, followed by frame boats, built like baskets and covered with animal skins and a coating of tar to keep the boat watertight. But it was the early logboats that allowed humans to conquer the Indo-Pacific. Over 6,000 years ago, the Polynesians used them to colonize all the Pacific islands. Hollowed from whole tree trunks, and with floats attached for stability, these so-called outriggers allowed them to navigate the wild seas thousands of years before the ocean-going explorers in their many-masted ships.

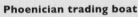

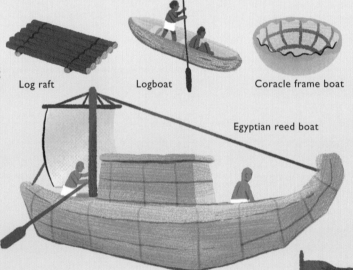

Log raft   Logboat   Coracle frame boat

Egyptian reed boat

4000 BCE

Most of the major cities in ancient Egypt were located along the River Nile. As a result, the Egyptians used the river for transportation and trade from the earliest times. They used reeds to build what were probably the first sailing boats. They had collapsible masts, allowing them to sail upstream using wind and then row back down with the current. The Egyptians developed many types of boat.s Some were specialised for fishing or traveling, while others were designed to carry cargo or for war.

Phoenician trading boat

Greek trireme

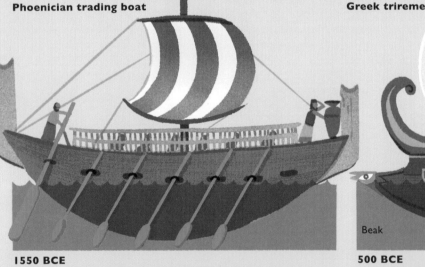

Cross-section

Beak

1550 BCE

The Phoenicians (people from the ancient civilization of Canaan—now Lebanon and Syria) used the galley, a man-powered sailing vessel, to travel, trade, and fight with their neighbors. With it, they became the greatest seafarers of the ancient world. This squat sailing vessel, rounded at both ends, was used for carrying goods and passengers, while a longer boat with a sharp battering ram for a bow was used for war.

500 BCE

To increase the speed of their boats, the Greeks needed to add more oarsmen. Rather than making their boats longer, which would make them structurally weak, they sat their oarsmen on three different levels to create a ship known as the trireme. Up to 170 men powered the heavy ships through the water. At their bow (front), they had an underwater beak made of bronze, which they rammed into enemy ships to sink them.

1000 CE

Viking longboats had sails as well as up to 60 oarsmen who rowed the ship. These boats were long and narrow so were able to travel along rivers as well as on the open sea, carrying the Vikings on their raids across the North Sea and even reaching North America. Sometimes extending to over 70 feet (20 m) long, these impressive ships were made from overlapping oak planks, with two high pointed ends, holes for sixteen oars along each side, and fittings for a broad oar to be worked as a rudder by the helmsman. A mast near the center carried a large rectangular sail.

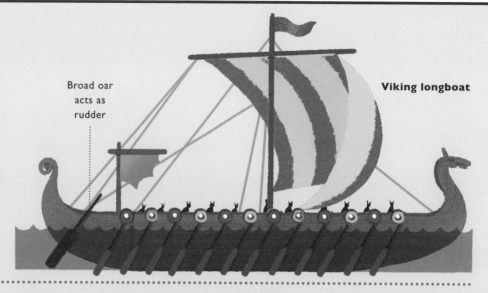

Broad oar acts as rudder

Viking longboat

Chinese junk

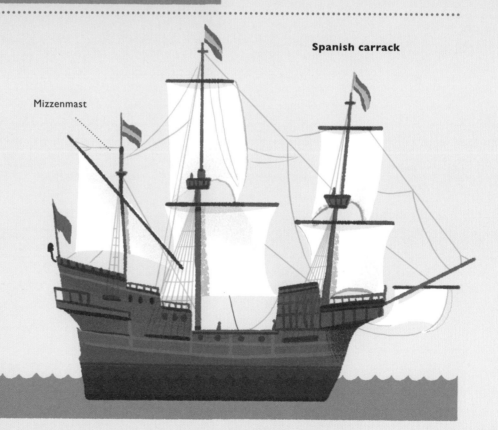

Sternpost rudder

1100 CE

The Chinese were the first people to build complex sails, which came in different shapes and sizes, and some could swing around to catch the direction of the wind. Chinese junks also had a number of other pioneering features later copied elsewhere, including the addition of the sternpost rudder to steer the boat—a large heavy board that could be lowered when the junk moved into deep water. Until this time, the conventional method of steering had been by means of a long oar projecting from the stern. Junks also had watertight compartments long before western ships. They were strong, easy to maneuver and were important boats for both war and trade. Some of the biggest were over 330 feet (100 m) long!

1450 CE onward

During the 15th century, boat design made many advancements, propelled by the need for bigger and more stable boats to explore the world's oceans—to discover new lands, go to battle, and carry cargo from country to country. The largest European sailing ship of these times was the three-masted Spanish carrack, weighing in at more than 1,000 tons and mainly used for carrying cargo. A carrack had rectangular sails on the main- and foremast but triangular sails on the mizzenmast (at the back), which could be moved to allow the boat to sail into the wind. The high deck at the bow (front) and stern (back) of the ship were called castles—the perfect place for lookouts or archers during battle. Lookouts could also climb to the so-called crow's nest at the top of the mainmast for an even better view.

Mizzenmast

Spanish carrack

THE MEDIEVAL WORLD

SEPARATING ANCIENT AND MODERN HISTORY IS A PERIOD OF HUMAN DEVELOPMENT SPANNING ROUGHLY A THOUSAND YEARS, FROM AROUND 400 TO 1500 CE. It begins after the fall of the Roman Empire, when many new smaller kingdoms arose in Europe and great empires grew in Arabia, Africa, India, and China.

In Europe, this time is called the medieval period or the Middle Ages, so called because it was the time between the end of imperial Rome and the start of the modern world. In the 14th century, it merged into the Renaissance, in which many discoveries took place that would change the course of human history yet again.

Elsewhere in the world, great civilizations such as the Incas and Aztecs flourished, largely unknown to Europeans. In the Far East, China grew prosperous under the rule of various imperial dynasties, and from India the Mongol Empire grew to become one of the largest the world has ever seen.

Toward the end of the period, in the years between 1400 and 1600 CE, European explorers brought whole continents into direct contact with each other for the first time. There were also great leaps forward in the areas of education, art, science, and architecture. This marked the start of modern history and the birth of the global world we know today.

476 – Western part of Roman Empire collapses; eastern part eventually becomes the Byzantine Empire

500 – Mayan civilization flourishes in Central America

555 – Byzantine Empire at its height

618 – Tang dynasty starts in China; paper money invented

632 – Islamic religion spreads after the death of Mohammed and the Islamic Empire is created

750 – Maoris reach New Zealand; Pueblo people begin to build villages in North America

840 – Viking seafarers spread out from Scandinavia

955 – Beginning of the Holy Roman Empire

960 – Song dynasty rules in China

CE

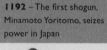

1350 – Renaissance begins in Italy

1368 – Ming dynasty of China begins

c.1300 – Ottoman Empire is founded in Turkey

1337 – Hundred Years' War begins between France and England

1347 – Black Death sweeps across Europe

1200 – The Silk Road trade route flourishes between China, India, and Europe

1206 – Genghis Khan unites Mongol tribes to form the Mongol Empire

1258 – End of the Islamic Empire

1291 – End of the Crusades

1192 – The first shogun, Minamoto Yoritomo, seizes power in Japan

c.1000 – Castle-building is at its height in Europe and the Middle East; Vikings reach North America

1096 – Start of the Crusades, when Christians fight Muslims for control of Jerusalem and the Holy Land

1400s – Inca Empire spreads in South America; Age of Exploration begins

1428 – Aztec empire rules in Mexico

c.1440 – Printing press is invented

1453 – Ottoman Empire stops trade on the Silk Road

1453 – Byzantine Empire conquered by Ottomans

1492 – Christopher Columbus lands in the Americas

1500s – The first African slaves are taken to work in the Americas, beginning the Atlantic slave trade

1517 – Martin Luther begins Protestant movement

1521 – Aztecs are conquered by Spanish invaders

1522 – First circumnavigation of the world, by Magellan

1526 – Mughal Empire founded in India

1532 – Inca Empire conquered by the conquistadors

1543 – Copernicus states that the Earth moves around the sun

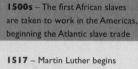

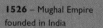

A PLACE OF WORSHIP

IN THE EARLY MIDDLE AGES, BELIEF IN THE GODS OF THE ANCIENT WORLD GRADUALLY WITHERED AWAY, and new religions emerged to take their place. Often these were based on the teachings of a single human individual rather than the belief in a pantheon of supernatural gods that had been common in the Old World. Between the 1st and 6th centuries CE, both Christianity and Islam were born and came to dominate much of the world in the centuries that followed. Buddhism too spread far from its roots in India to become the main religion of the East.

Over time, many of the main religions splintered into smaller groups—Christians, for example, split into Roman Catholics, Protestants, Lutherans, and Calvinists to name just a few. By the end of the Middle Ages, these new religions stood alongside those that had survived from older times (such as Hinduism) to form a complex web of different beliefs across the world.

As before, worshippers erected buildings in honor of their gods—churches and cathedrals, mosques, temples, and synagogues. Many of the most impressive buildings of medieval times are those built in the name of worship, from the great churches of Europe to the temples of the East. Some now lie in ruins, testament to the great struggles of these times, when people from one religion fought another. Others were adopted by another religion, with different decoration or features added or taken away to make the building fit the new set of beliefs. Like the cathedral of Hagia Sophia shown here, these great buildings often carry the history of the religious world in their very stones.

The Hagia Sophia, whose name means "holy wisdom," is a domed monument originally built in Constantinople (now Istanbul, Turkey) in the 6th century on the site of a pagan temple. Constructed on the orders of Justinian I, emperor of Byzantium, the building was completed in the remarkably short time of about six years. It served first as a Christian orthodox cathedral during the Byzantine Empire, was looted during the Crusades when it was briefly turned into a Roman Catholic church, and then from 1453 became an imperial Islamic mosque. Its interiors have had many different rich decorations over the years, including beautiful mosaics of different religious scenes, imperial portraits, monograms of the Muslim caliphs (religious leaders), and images depicting the life of Jesus Christ. Islamic features—such as the four minarets—were added when it was repurposed as a mosque under the Ottomans. It was the world's largest place of worship for nearly a thousand years, before being turned into a museum in 1935.

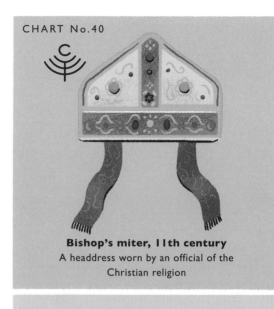

Bishop's miter, 11th century
A headdress worn by an official of the
Christian religion

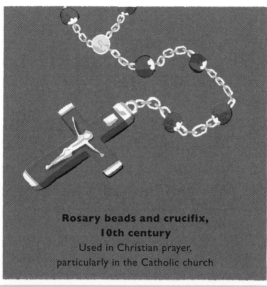

**Rosary beads and crucifix,
10th century**
Used in Christian prayer,
particularly in the Catholic church

Prayer wheel, 5th century
A revolving cylinder inscribed with prayers
used by Tibetan Buddhists

HOLY OBJECTS

ALL RELIGIONS INVOLVE RITUAL, whether talking to a god in prayer, making offerings at a temple, or coming together in worship with others. Sometimes religions involve ceremonies that may include reading from a sacred book, singing and dancing, or perhaps simply sitting in quiet meditation or receiving a blessing.

Often these rituals involve the use of holy objects, beautifully crafted by human hands in honor of their gods—statues of the gods themselves, elaborate shrines where candles can be lit or offerings left, simple jewelry worn as a symbol of the wearer's belief, or richly decorated costumes worn by holy men or women.

Whatever the religion, for centuries humans have created objects of staggering beauty in the name of worship.

Menorah, 12th century
A many-branching candelabrum
used in Jewish worship

Reliquary shrine, 14th century
This would contain the relics of a saint.

Hindu shankha, 11th century
A conch shell of ritual and religious
importance in Hinduism,
often used as a ceremonial trumpet.

Byzantine icon, 11th century
A religious work of art, often used
as part of religious meditation or prayer.

Qu'ran, 13th century
The holy book of Islam

Statue of Buddha, 7th century
The central figure of the Buddhist religion,
founded in the 5th century BCE

LIFE IN A MEDIEVAL TOWN

THROUGHOUT EUROPE DURING MUCH OF THE MIDDLE AGES, SOCIETY WAS ORGANIZED VERY DIFFERENTLY FROM THE WAY WE LIVE TODAY. People were divided into four main groups—the kings, the nobles, the knights, and the peasants—each with their own jobs to do. In each kingdom, all the land belonged to the king and was granted by him to various nobles. In exchange, they had to swear loyalty to the king and agree to provide him with soldiers for his army. The nobles in turn gave land to their knights as payment for their help in battle. Each knight let peasants live on his land, but they were essentially owned by him and had to give him the lion's share of their produce.

Life in most small communities revolved around the local lord or knight and his manor or fief. The lord controlled the land and everything in it, including most of the people. He lived in a large house or castle with his family and servants, surrounded by a small village and, beyond that, by farmland that was worked by the peasants, known as serfs or villeins.

This way of structuring society later became known as feudalism, and was the basis of the medieval class system. It defined the "haves" and the "have-nots" and kept the majority of the population in conditions of near slavery while using them to provide the resources needed by all.

• Most people living in the Middle Ages were peasants, about 90 percent of the population in western Europe. They had a hard life, owned virtually nothing, worked hard, and most died before they reached the age of 30.

• The local lord held absolute power over his manor, including setting punishments for crimes.

• In the late Middle Ages, laws were passed, called "sumptuary" laws, to ensure that the class structure was maintained. Among other things, these laws stated who could wear what types of clothes and what materials they could use to make them.

• Toward the end of the medieval period, a new class started to arise—the merchants, who accumulated wealth and power through trade and the provision of services—as well as a new subdivision of the clergy: intellectuals trained in literature and writing. By the end of the Middle Ages, feudalism had begun to wane due to warfare, disease, and political change.

King

Nobles

Knights

THE SOCIAL PYRAMID OF POWER

Surfs

Church

In most of Europe, the medieval Church was very powerful and also very wealthy. As well as receiving a tithe (tax) of 10 percent of everyone's income, they received money for services like christenings and funerals. People also paid penances for wrongdoing, believing they would never get to heaven otherwise. Some people gave land to the Church to gain God's favor—about 30 percent of all the land in Western Europe belonged to the Catholic church during the Middle Ages.

Farming

Most farmers during the Middle Ages planted their crops in rotation. Villages usually had three fields—one planted with wheat, one with barley, and one left fallow (unplanted) so it would have time to recover and be ready for planting the next year. Each field was divided into strips for different families to farm. The serfs also had gardens where they grew vegetables, herbs, and fruits and sometimes kept a few animals, such as chickens for eggs and cows for milk and cheese.

Freemen

Not all peasants were required to work the land. Some, called freemen, ran their own businesses, such as carpenters, bakers, and blacksmiths, and provided services in return for food. They were not bound to the manor like the serfs, and could take their services to other parts of the country. If they chose to stay, they paid a fixed rent to the lord (either in money or produce) in exchange for using his land. Some freemen became landowners themselves and even became wealthy through their industry.

Buildings

Peasants lived in small, timber-framed houses of one or two rooms. Living conditions were crowded, dark, and usually uncomfortable with everyone sleeping together in one room. Animals, such as cows or sheep, often lived inside the home as well. There was no glass in the windows, an open fire was the only source of heat, and all the water had to be fetched from the village well or local river or stream. In contrast, the lord and his family lived in the big manor house along with their servants, who fetched everything they needed.

Clothing and possessions

Most peasants wore plain clothing made from heavy wool to keep them warm during the winter. They had very little in the way of possessions—a few pieces of basic furniture and perhaps a few homemade goods. In contrast, nobles wore clothes made from fine wool, velvet, and even silk. They had many possessions depending on their wealth—tapestries to hang on the walls, fine furniture, and precious objects brought from foreign lands.

Food

Wealthy nobles insisted on all vegetables and fruits being cooked, as it was thought that raw foods could make you ill! They also ate a vast variety of meat and game, including venison, beef, pork, goat, lamb, rabbit, hare, swan, heron, and poultry, as well as fish. Often, these dishes would be flavored with expensive spices like ginger, pepper, and nutmeg, which were imported from abroad. In contrast, peasants mostly ate bread and vegetable stews made of beans, dried peas, and cabbage. All people mostly drank ale or wine since water was often contaminated and could make them sick.

Towns

Life in medieval towns was very different from life in the country. People living there paid rent to the local lord, but they did not have to work for him and could choose how to earn their living. Many were craftworkers, making goods like clothing or pottery to sell to other townspeople. Others made a living as merchants, selling wool or wood, or trading in goods from foreign lands, such as silk and spices. Towns were a center of trade so other occupations also sprang up to provide services, such as innkeepers, bakers, butchers, and doctors.

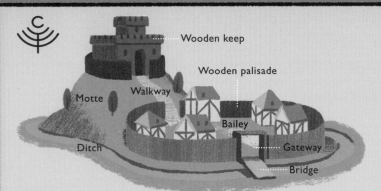

Motte-and-bailey castle

The earliest castle design was a wooden keep built on top of a huge mound of earth (the motte). Around the motte was a steep-sided ditch often surrounded with a wooden fence, later replaced by a stone wall. The lord lived on the upper floor of the keep for protection; everyone else lived in a fenced-off area at ground level known as the bailey, connected to the motte by a bridge or walkway.

STONE KEEPS

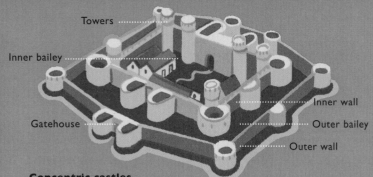

Stone keeps

As time passed, wooden keeps were replaced by longer-lasting ones made of stone. Early stone keeps were square in shape but this design had weaknesses—the corners had blind spots where attackers could creep up unnoticed and, although the single entrance made it hard for attackers to get in, it also made it hard for anyone inside to get out. Over the next 200 years, keeps became round and huge stone walls with gatehouses were built around the bailey and keep. The whole thing was surrounded by a great ditch of water called a moat and access was controlled by a drawbridge, which could be raised if the castle was under siege, and a fortified iron gate called a portcullis, which could be lowered against attackers.

Concentric castles

In the 13th century, an important new castle design was brought back to Europe by the Crusaders fighting in the Middle East. These castles had no weak spots. For defense, two walls ran around the outside—the inner wall was higher so the defenders could easily fire down on any attackers over the heads of the soldiers guarding the outer wall. Lookout towers on the walls stood far out from the corners so there were no blind spots. These concentric castles had comfortable living quarters built around a central courtyard.

CASTLES

DURING THE MIDDLE AGES, PEOPLE HAD TO BE PREPARED FOR WAR AT ANY TIME. Kings and nobles built castles to protect themselves—great military strongholds in which they lived with their families, servants, and soldiers, designed to be easy to defend. The earliest castles, called motte-and-bailey castles, could be built quickly and cheaply, but over time they were replaced by huge, longer-lasting stone-built castles.

The castle was the center of things—from there the lord of the castle managed his surrounding lands and all the peasants under his control, kept law and order, trained his knights and foot soldiers ready for battle, and held feasts and tournaments to keep everyone happy.

LIVING IN A CASTLE

Keep

Solar—living quarters
for the lord and lady

Bedroom

Chapel

Great
hall

Minstrel

Guards' room

Garderobe
(toilet)

Storeroom

Kitchen

Dungeon

Tournaments

The lord of the castle would often arrange mock battles, or tournaments, to be held in the castle grounds for the amusement of his people. Jousting was the most popular sport at such events where knights would challenge each other for a prize.

The great hall

During lavish feasts in the great hall, there would be lots of entertainment—singing, dancing, music, even jesters, acrobats, and magicians. Many courses of food could mean the feast lasted for several hours.

A CASTLE UNDER SIEGE

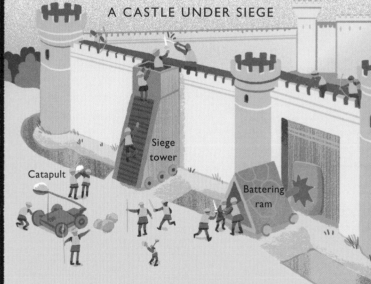

Siege
tower

Catapult

Battering
ram

Although castles were designed to be easy to defend, new forms of weapon were invented that could cause them great damage. Battering rams could break open the entrance, siege towers could be used to climb on to the outer walls, and huge wooden catapults, known as trebuchets, could be used to hurl rocks at the castle walls. One of the most effective ways of taking control of a castle was to surround it so no one could leave or enter, and simply starve the occupants into submission.

WARS AND WARRIORS

HUMANS HAVE ALWAYS WAGED WAR AGAINST EACH OTHER. For over 5,000 years, since the rise of the first civilizations, they have fought with their neighbors over land or resources, tried to overthrow their rulers, or defeat those of a different race or religious belief. All over the world, great empires have grown through conquest, winning more and more land and imposing their rules over others, only to eventually be defeated in turn. Primitive wars were seldom well organized and their participants rarely had any specialized training in the art of fighting, but as our societies evolved so too did our ability to fight with one another. Rulers built up huge armies, filled with men trained to battle to the death for their cause, armed with increasingly complicated weapons and protected by elaborate suits of armor.

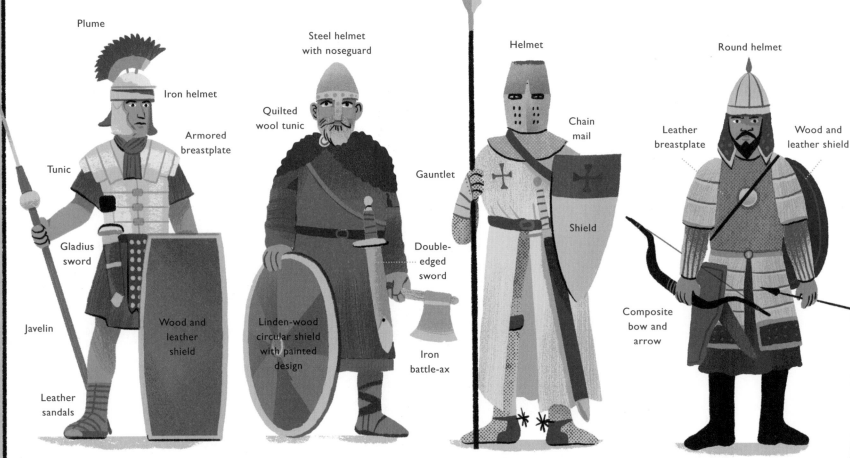

Roman soldier, c.100 CE
The efficiency of their army was largely responsible for the success of the Roman empire, which, at its height in the 1st century, stretched over most of the known world, from Asia Minor to Portugal and from North Africa to Scotland. The army was organized into groups of highly trained foot soldiers, known as legionaries. Every soldier had armor to protect their upper body, shoulders, and head, and carried many weapons, including two javelins, a short sword known as a gladius, and a dagger.

Viking raider, c.780 CE
For over 300 years from the late 8th century CE, Viking raiders terrorized the people of northern Europe, setting sail from Scandinavia in their great longships in search of new territory. They attacked settlements along the coast, fighting their way inland, and carrying off treasure and slaves. Vikings were skilled metalworkers, making helmets of hammered steel lined with cloth and held on by leather straps. Their weapons included broad battle-axes and large knives that doubled as tools for everyday use. They relied on wooden shields for defense, and thick clothing of wool or hemp.

Crusader, c.1140 CE
In the 11th century, the head of the Roman Catholic Church, Pope Urban II, called for a crusade, or Holy War, to capture Jerusalem from its Muslim rulers. So began the Crusades that lasted for nearly 200 years. The Crusaders came from all walks of life—some were pilgrims, others were wealthy knights. Most of the knights wore metal helms (helmets), shields, an array of weapons, and a coat of chain mail, made of small overlapping links of iron, which could ward off the point of a dagger or the thrust of a spear or sword.

Mongol warrior, c.1250 CE
During the 13th century, the Mongols carved out a vast empire that stretched across much of Central Asia, Persia, and China. Led by their chief Genghis Khan, they undertook a series of conquests that killed tens of millions of people, but by the end of the century, their empire had collapsed. The Mongol warriors were only lightly armored, with metal helmets and breastplates made from small rectangular plates of iron, leather, or bronze, but they were famous as skilled horsemen, astonishing archers, clever battle tacticians, and cruel and ruthless fighters.

Land of the samurai

For hundreds of years, Japan was controlled by a series of military dictators known as shoguns. They controlled an aristocratic class of warriors known as the samurai who became famous for their bravery and skill. They prized loyalty above all things, and a samurai would rather commit ritual suicide (known as seppuku or hara-kiri) than suffer any dishonor. Samurai warriors wore a suit of armor made of many pieces of bamboo or hardened leather laced together with silk ties and gold detailing.

KINGS VERSUS KINGS

From 1337 to 1453, England repeatedly invaded France, fighting wars over who owned land, a period that became known as the Hundred Years' War. Though it was a small, poor country, in the beginning England won most of the battles, largely because its army was well disciplined and successfully used the newly developed longbows to stop cavalry charges. By this time, wealthy knights could afford to go to battle dressed in a made-to-measure full suit of armor, formed from overlapping metal plates. However, at the Battle of Castillon in 1453, everything changed when the French introduced cannons and guns to the field of battle and used them to devastating effect against the English. Over the next hundred years, the knights in their suits of shiny armor gradually became obsolete, castles proved worthless because cannons could take down their walls and guns gradually became the weapon of choice on battlefields the world over.

A SUIT OF 15TH CENTURY ARMOR

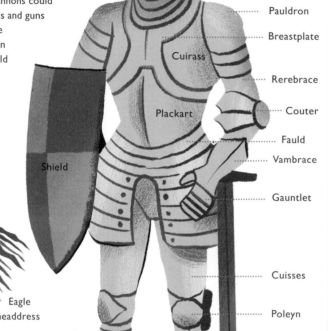

- Comb
- Helmet
- Visor
- Pauldron
- Breastplate
- Cuirass
- Rerebrace
- Plackart
- Couter
- Fauld
- Vambrace
- Shield
- Gauntlet
- Cuisses
- Poleyn
- Sword
- Greave
- Spurs
- Sabaton

SPANISH CONQUISTADOR

EAGLE WARRIOR

- Helmet
- Leather face guard
- Steel sword
- Obsidian flakes
- Club
- Leather armor
- Samurai sword
- Arquebus (gun)
- Eagle headdress
- Bamboo staves tied around legs

End of the Aztecs

The Aztec society of central Mexico was built around warfare. Aztecs fought neighboring tribes for food, treasure, and to widen their rule, but also to take captives (thousands of them) that could be sacrificed to appease their gods. Warriors dressed in relation to their success on the battlefield—the most successful were eagle warriors who wore clothing covered in feathers and a feathered helmet that included an open beak. For armor, they relied on quilted cotton soaked in brine, which, when dried, was more resistant to damage by blade or spear. Aztec warriors had various weapons at their disposal—slings, poison-tipped darts for use in blowpipes, bows and arrows, atlatls (spear-throwers), and clubs edged with razor-sharp pieces of obsidian (volcanic glass), but none could help them in the face of invasion by the Conquistadors, who arrived from Spain in 1519 determined to conquer the Aztec people. Terrified of the Spanish crossbows, guns, and horses, none of which the Aztec people had ever seen before, they were soon defeated. Many also died from the spread of European diseases, and their way of life soon disappeared.

EUROPEAN ARMOR THROUGH THE AGES

| 500 BCE | 100 BCE | 800 | 1066 | 1200s | 1300s | 1400s | 1500s | 1600s |

WEAPONS OF WAR

HUMANKIND HAS ALWAYS HAD NEED OF WEAPONS. Faced with an enemy or a wild animal, early humans could strike out with a wooden club or throw a stone to defend themselves. Later they learned to make spears or shoot arrows with a bow. Many of these early weapons were used primarily to hunt animals for food. However, as human societies grew, their weapons were increasingly used against other humans, fighting to gain land or resources, to overthrow rulers, or challenge those of a different race or religious belief.

The quality of weaponry was greatly improved by the discovery of metals, which allowed for the creation of a whole new range of arms, far more durable, deadly, and reliable than the early ones fashioned from wood, stone, and bone. By the medieval period, warriors around the world had a huge variety

of swords, lances, axes, and other weaponry to help them fight their battles. Then, in the 14th century, the invention of firearms changed the face of warfare forever.

• While there were many variations of weapon, they mostly fell into a couple of categories. First were those used for hand-to-hand combat, like swords, daggers, spears, axes, pole-arms (essentially spears with ax-like heads), hammers, or clubs. They had either sharp edges for cutting, sharp points for thrusting, heavy heads for crushing, or sometimes a combination of all three. Second were missile weapons that were designed to be thrown or shot from farther away, like slings, spears, arrows, and javelins. Some, such as spears, served for both throwing and thrusting.

• Battle tactics were also important in the effective use of

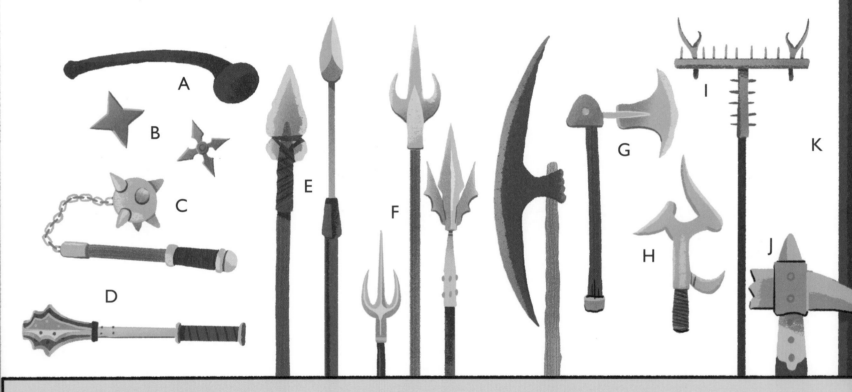

KEY TO ILLUSTRATION

A. **Knobkerrie**—A short stick with a knob at one end, traditionally used as a club by the indigenous peoples of South Africa.

B. **Shuriken**—Used mostly by samurai warriors, the word shuriken means "dagger in the hand." These sharp blades could be thrown with great force at an enemy.

C. **Flail**—A spiked ball-and-chain used by medieval warriors.

D. **Mace**—A short club with a heavy head used to break through armor, and to deliver crushing blows. Similar weapons covered with spikes were known as morning stars.

E. **Spears**—Made from a simple shaft with a pointed head, spears have been crafted from a variety of materials and used in virtually every culture since Neolithic times. Some, such as javelins, were used along with a throwing strap to increase range.

F. **Pole Arms**—Many different types of pole arm were created for use in battle. Some were extremely long with three-pronged blades or spear tips for use against mounted cavalry. Pikes, thick spears with pointed heads that could reach over 6 feet (2 m) in length were used by groups of soldiers fighting shoulder to shoulder and were impenetrable to enemy cavalry. Bardiches ended in a curved blade and were used in Eastern Europe and Scandinavia until

the 16th century.

G. **Battle-ax**—Used from prehistoric times to the 1600s, these axes came in countless variations and sizes, and were made from many materials including stone, wood and metal.

H. **Mambele**—An African knife, also known as a hunga-munga, that could be used as a thrown weapon as well as for fighting at close quarters.

I. **Sodegarami**—A spiked pole used in medieval Japan that could entangle the fabric of a kimono to bring down an

enemy without harming them. It was useful for disabling samurai warriors who legally couldn't be harmed.

J. **War hammer**—Designed to combat steel armor, this vicious weapon could be used to crush or gouge an opponent.

K. **Pole-ax**—Over time the basic ax began to evolve, gaining an armor-piercing spike on the back and another on the end for thrusting. The resulting pole-ax could break through armor and could operate as an ax blade, a back-spike, and a hammer. It was

weapons. A lone spearman, for example, wouldn't stand a chance if his sword-bearing enemy got too close, so usually spearmen stood shoulder to shoulder, several ranks deep, to protect each other when attacking their enemies.

• The introduction of horses to the battlefield also led to the use of new weapons. The spear was lengthened to form the lance, the chief weapon of the mounted soldier from the fall of the Roman Empire until the late Middle Ages.

• As missile weapons got bigger and stronger, they changed the ways that wars were fought. The three-foot-long (meter-long) arrows shot from a longbow could pierce even the toughest armor, and such was their range that banks of archers could rain a storm of arrows onto the charging horsemen of their enemies from a distance of over 650 feet (200 m).

• The coming of gunpowder, first invented in 9th-century China by alchemists who were attempting to make an elixir of immortality, led to huge changes in missile weaponry, particularly the invention of

firearms. These followed the same principle as that of blowpipes, only using gunpowder to shoot the missile out of its tube rather than human lung-power, and came to replace many of the weapons of war that had come before.

• The first guns were cannons, used in battles from the early 14th century onward. For many years, nearly all cannons were extremely inefficient—although they made a lot of noise, they had a very short range (distance) and were so unsafe that they often burst, killing more of their own soldiers than those of the enemy.

• Similarly, many difficulties had to be overcome in the development of handguns—such as finding an effective method of lighting the gunpowder while at the same time taking aim, a task that often required two soldiers working together and a degree of concentration difficult to find while in the throes of battle. The first effective mechanism to solve this was the matchlock. This used a fuse to light the powder, thereby allowing the firer several seconds between the fuse being lit and the gunpowder exploding—when he could steady his weapon and take aim.

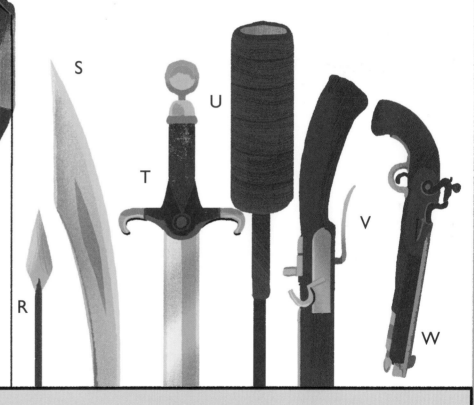

the favored weapon for men-at-arms fighting on foot into the 16th century.

L. **Haladie**—A double-edged blade used by the warriors of ancient India.

M. **Triple dagger**—A three-bladed knife used in the Middle Ages. By pressing a button, two extra spring-loaded blades could be made to fly out, to devastating effect when used in close combat.

N. **Stiletto**—Also called a misericorde (meaning "mercy"), this dagger gained fame during the Middle Ages as the secondary

weapon of knights.

O. **Bagh nakh**—A claw-like weapon from India designed to fit over the knuckles or be concealed against the palm and consisting of a number of curved blades fixed to a crossbar.

P. **Katar**—A push dagger from Southeast Asia. Its distinctive H-shaped hand grip causes the blade to sit above the user's knuckles.

Q. **Longbow**—Standing as tall as its shooter, the longbow dominated battlefields from the Bronze Age to the 1600s.

R. **Composite bow**—Made from horn, wood, and sinew, these bows could fire arrows a great distance for their size, making them especially useful for mounted archery. The design first originated among the nomad tribes of Asia and spread among the military of most civilizations that came into contact with them.

S. **Scimitar**—With its long, curved blade, the scimitar was the iconic weapon of soldiers throughout the Middle East for hundreds of years from the 13th-

century Ottoman period.

T. **Longsword**—These European double-edged swords were popular in the late medieval and Renaissance periods.

U. **Hand cannon**—The forerunner of the handgun, widely used in China and later throughout Europe until the 1500s when it was supplanted by the matchlock arquebus. It was fired by holding a burning wick to a "touch hole" in the barrel that ignited the powder inside.

V. **Arquebus**—A type of matchlock, the first firearm to

have a mechanical trigger for firing. Matchlocks appeared in Europe in the mid-15th century and by the 16th century were widely used. In battle, lines of soldiers would be used to fire volleys of musket balls at the enemy, which proved much more effective than single soldiers trying to hit individual targets.

W. **Flintlock pistol**—Invented some time in the late 1500s. Fired using the spark from a flint, an ignition system that reigned for two centuries with virtually no alteration.

SIEGE WEAPONS

IMAGINE YOU HAVE BEATEN YOUR ENEMY ON THE BATTLEFIELD, but now the survivors have taken cover behind the walls of their great castle. You could cut off all supplies, then simply wait for the inhabitants to surrender, but that could mean a long wait. The alternative was to invent a new class of weaponry that could help you break into even the greatest stronghold. Known as siege engines, these weapons could be used to wage war on an enemy fortification from outside.

• Some siege weapons weren't just used to hurl rocks and stones. Diseased animals, dead bodies, or even rotting food were hurled over the castle walls as a form of bio-weapon, to spread disease or make the starving people inside so ill that they would surrender more quickly.

• Fire played an important part in siege warfare. It was used to burn wooden supports out from underneath walls, or sent into the fortification on flaming arrows. Smoke was also used as a weapon and soldiers would often make special projectiles loaded with noxious substances (like chicken droppings or poisonous plants), which helped turn the smoke cloud into a kind of tear gas.

• Despite the methods available for breaking a siege the attackers—aware of a prolonged siege's great cost in time, money, and lives—would sometimes offer generous terms for a quick surrender to their enemies.

Onager—A catapult that used bundles of tightly wound rope, horse, or even human hair that, when released, hurled a projectile up and over a castle or city walls. Simple to build, use, and reload, the onager was a staple of Roman siege warfare for millennia.

Ballista—Like a giant crossbow on wheels, ballistas could fire giant arrows or stone "cannonballs" to hammer a castle wall to pieces.

Trebuchets—Giant catapults, trebuchets often required a hundred men or more to operate them. They relied on a heavy counterweight to send the long arm upward and sling the load far into the distance. They were also used to launch great fireballs—stones wrapped in hay soaked in tar, then set alight.

Battering ram—Usually made from a huge log suspended on ropes and covered by a roof to protect its operators from arrow fire, these rams were used to batter down walls or gates.

Cannons—These changed the rules of warfare almost overnight and so altered the course of history. In 1453, the Ottomans used enormous cannons like this to break down the walls of the Byzantine city of Constantinople, thought to be unbreakable for more than a thousand years.

Counter-weight

Sling

Projectile

Pouch

Siege tower—These glorified ladders could be wheeled up to the walls of castles, thereby allowing the invaders to quickly climb up and over the top. The sight of a line of massive siege towers was often enough to encourage surrender before the battle had even began.

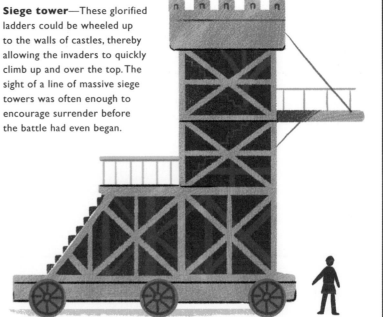

SLAVERY

SLAVERY, THE OWNERSHIP OF ONE PERSON BY ANOTHER, HAS EXISTED SINCE ANCIENT TIMES. Human slaves could be bought and sold in the same way as any other piece of property and were obliged to carry out whatever work was required of them. Although some eventually gained their freedom or rebelled against their owners, most died while still enslaved. Their living conditions were usually brutal and their lives short.

• Both the Sumerians and ancient Egyptians kept slaves but the practice reached its height in the ancient world under the Greeks and Romans.

• In ancient Greece, slaves made most of the goods, and were put to work in homes and on farms.

• In Rome, many were made to fight in the Roman army, or were trained as gladiators to fight for the amusement of the public. Slaves trained as gladiators in Rome could earn their freedom by distinguishing themselves during fights. One famous slave, Spartacus, led a revolt of slaves against the Romans in 73 BCE. The slaves were defeated, and 6,000

of them were crucified.

• The act of an owner freeing a slave was known as manumission. This was usually in recognition of years of good and faithful service and often the freed slave was still required to perform duties for his master.

• Slaves were often sold in special slave markets that could be found in many towns and cities throughout the world. Potential buyers could examine the "merchandise," who were often made to stand naked with their wrists bound together, to make sure they were in good health.

• In Europe, the demand for slaves grew after the Black Death of the 14th century, which decimated much of the European workforce. Early traders from Portugal brought slaves from the west coast of Africa back to Europe in the early 1400s and so began a terrible trade in human beings that lasted for more than 400 years. Vast numbers of Africans, perhaps over 7 million individuals, were sold by Europeans for profit, shipped across the Atlantic to work as slaves in the newly created cotton and tobacco plantations and other colonies around the world.

A CAMEL CARAVAN OF SLAVES
ARRIVING AT AN ARAB SLAVE MARKET, c.1400 CE

MAKING MEDICINE

TODAY, WE KNOW A LOT ABOUT THE HUMAN BODY, how to prevent diseases, heal wounds, and diagnose illnesses, but this is a comparatively recent skill. Medical science as we know it began only about 300 years ago. Before this, humans had very little real medical knowledge, and much of what they did know was often more concerned with magic than medicine.

In some ancient cultures, doctors were also priests, treating people according to the rules laid down in their sacred books, or reading signs in everything from burnt bones to animal entrails. It took us thousands of years to begin to understand illnesses and to develop the means to treat and prevent them.

• Among many ancient cultures cures involved spells, charms, and protective amulets, as well as herbal remedies. Even the ancient Egyptians, who studied medicine and learned much about the uses of drugs, believed that many illnesses were sent by the gods, a common belief among many ancient civilizations.

• Medical knowledge took a leap forward with the great thinkers of ancient Greece. Greek doctors first coined the expression "diagnosis" for the process of assessing a patient's symptoms and, like a detective, arriving at a conclusion as to the cause of the complaint, although they still blamed the gods for many illnesses.

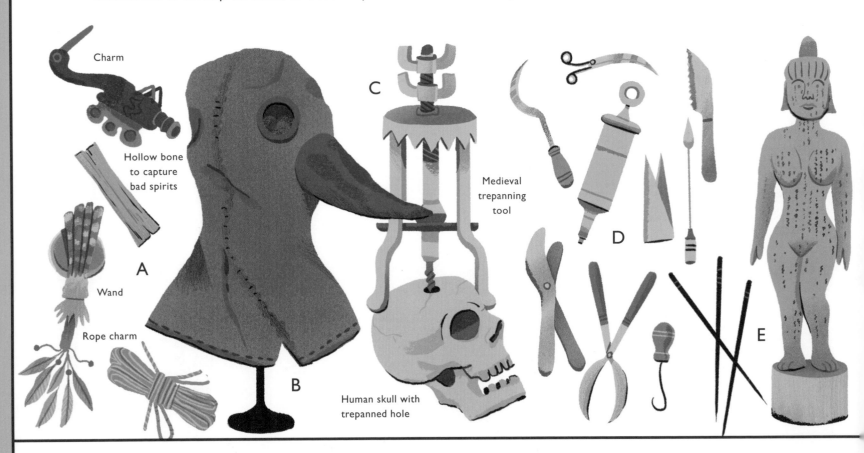

Charm

Hollow bone to capture bad spirits

Wand

Rope charm

A

B

C

Medieval trepanning tool

Human skull with trepanned hole

D

E

KEY TO ILLUSTRATION

A. Shaman tools, c.1500

In many ancient societies spirits were believed to make their presence known through disease and the only person who could cure illness was the shaman. Treatments often involved ritual chanting or sacrifice, as well as herbs. A shaman usually wore special robes or masks, and used rattles, drums, and charms in order to affect a cure.

B. Plague mask, c.1650

Little was understood about the plagues of the Middle Ages, but some believed that the disease could be passed on through smell. Some plague doctors wore special garments to help protect them, including a mask with glass eye openings and a beak-shaped nose stuffed with straw, strongly scented herbs, and spices such as ambergris, lemon balm, mint, cloves, and rose petals.

C. Trepanning tool, c.1500

One type of medical treatment can be traced back to prehistoric times. In a form of surgery known as trepanning, a small round hole was drilled into or cut out of a patient's skull, to release the disease or evil spirit causing the pain. Hundreds of such skulls have been found all over the world, an indication that such painful operations were widespread. Different tools were invented to help keep the patient in place during the procedure.

D. Surgeons' knives, c.1000 BCE

With no pain control and a high risk of infection, surgery in ancient times was painful and dangerous. Yet nearly 3,000 years ago, skilled surgeons in India were performing operations with surgical instruments very much like those we use today, including scalpels, scissors, saws, needles, and forceps. They amputated limbs, removed cataracts, and even gave people new noses!

E Acupuncture needles and model, c.1650

Chinese physicians began using acupuncture thousands of years ago, aiming to cure diseases and ease pain by pushing tiny needles into areas of the body. Early needles were made of bone. The ones shown here come from the Qing dynasty and were made of metal, carried in a wooden case. The statue shows some of the acupuncture points on the human body.

• By the Middle Ages, medical treatments throughout much of Europe were still hampered by ignorance and superstition. In contrast, the caliphs (rulers) of the Persian Empire welcomed learned doctors from all over the world to research and discuss medicine, building on the work of the ancient Greeks. Islamic cities such as Baghdad and Cairo possessed the world's most advanced hospitals, and their scholars later made important discoveries, including an understanding of the circulation of the blood. The Islamic religion also contained rules about hygiene and diet, recognizing that cleanliness was important in maintaining good health.

• Without antiseptics and anesthetics, medieval surgery was an act of last resort. Most surgeons of the time were barbers who performed surgical operations alongside their other duties, which included bloodletting and taking out teeth!

• It would not be until the end of the Renaissance that the world of medicine would start to resemble the one we know today, with huge breakthroughs in our understanding of the human body and how it works.

FLEGMAT SANGVIN

MELANC COLERIC

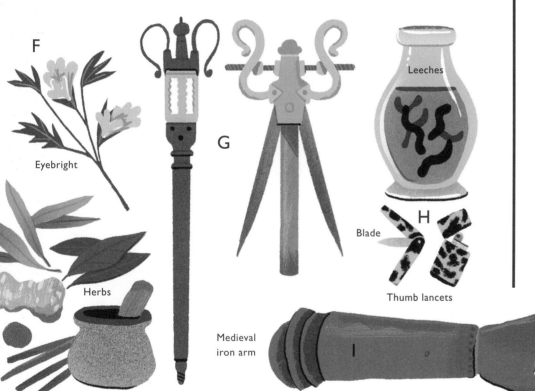

Eyebright

Herbs

Leeches

Blade

H

Thumb lancets

G

Medieval iron arm

I

J

A DIAGRAM OF THE "FOUR HUMORS"

The idea that all living things are made up of four elements—earth, air, fire, and water—was first proposed by the ancient Greeks. In the 2nd century, it was applied to humans. The body was thought to be composed of four humors, or liquids—blood, phlegm, black bile (choler), and yellow bile (melancholy). These humors had to be balanced in just the right quantities. If one lessened or increased, then the person would become ill. The belief in this system was widely held by doctors and other learned people throughout the Middle Ages, dominating medical thought for 1,400 years.

F. **Herbs**
During the Middle Ages, sick people often sought herbal cures from healers such as wise women, who provided treatment based on the belief that God had left "signatures" to show that certain plants, resembling parts of the human body, could be used to cure illnesses that arose there. Eyebright, for example, was used to treat eye infections because the flower supposedly looked like an eye.

G. **Extraction tools, c.1500s**
As humans invented new weapons to injure and kill each other, so doctors had to find new ways of treating the wounded. The tool on the right was used for removing arrow heads from deep wounds. The tool on the left is a bullet extractor. It was placed in the wound, and the screw lengthened using the handle at the top in order to pierce the bullet and remove it.

H. **Bloodletting tools, c.1400s**
Bloodletting was a common medical practice until the late 19th century to cure or prevent illness or disease by achieving the right balance of blood in the body. Patients could be "bled" by being cut by a thumb lancet like this, where the sharp blade was protected by a hinged cover of tortoiseshell, or by using leeches to draw out the "bad blood" that medieval physicians believed to cause many ailments.

I. **Prosthetic arm, c.1500**
The earliest example of a prosthesis (false body part) is a 3,000-year-old toe, made of wood, that belonged to an Egyptian noblewoman. The first recorded wearer of a false arm was a Roman general who lost his right hand in battle and was given one made of iron so he could continue fighting. In the early 16th century, advances in the development of prosthetic limbs were made with the invention of hinged hands and legs.

J. **Hamsa amulet, c.1600**
Amulets and talismans were, and for some people still are, objects thought to have magical or spiritual powers, bringing the wearer protection from bad luck and illness. This hamsa amulet, depicting an open hand, was used in the Middle East and Africa as a sign of protection and to provide defense against the evil eye. Amulets such as this were often prescribed by healers alongside herbal remedies.

THE BLACK DEATH

IN THE 14TH CENTURY, A DEADLY EPIDEMIC THAT LATER BECAME KNOWN AS THE BLACK DEATH SWEPT ACROSS EUROPE, carried along the great trading routes by the fleas living on rats. It was bubonic plague, a disease that usually causes death within just a few days of infection. In medieval times, plagues happened fairly regularly, but the death toll for this outbreak was unprecedented. In just four years, it killed around 20 to 30 million people, and in so doing changed the course of human history.

• The Black Death starts with a fever and progresses with vomiting, coughing, sneezing, and problems breathing. A rash of red and black spots covers the body along with painful lumps, known as buboes, in the armpits and groin. Most people died in one or two days but some lasted six days in total agony. Very few people survived.

• It is caused by a kind of bacteria that lives in fleas and is thought to have first been caught by black rats in Asia. Because there were so many rats in the medieval world—scavenging on sailing ships and infesting the crowded, dirty towns and cities—it spread very quickly along trading routes, passing to humans when fleas carrying the bacteria bit them. By 1350, most of Europe was infected.

• There was no cure for the plague, as antibiotics had yet to be invented. However, some people tried to protect themselves by carrying around sweet-smelling bundles of flowers or herbs, or trying herbal remedies or bleeding by leeches. Others thought the plague was a punishment from God and whipped themselves in the streets to show repentance for their sins.

• In some places, the houses of plague carriers were marked with a cross on the door to warn others to keep away. In many towns, there were so many bodies that they were collected in carts and buried in mass graves.

• Ironically, the Black Death did eventually make life better—for the survivors! So many people died that there was a shortage of labor, which gave peasants bargaining power with their masters. The Black Death played a part in the breakdown of the feudal system in Europe, giving the poor better wages and treatment.

SPREAD OF THE PLAGUE

1347 1349
1348 1350

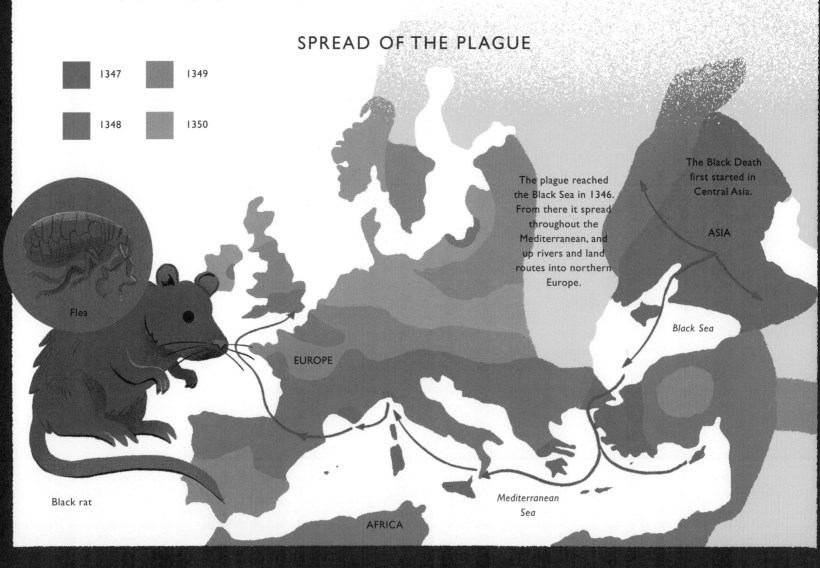

The plague reached the Black Sea in 1346. From there it spread throughout the Mediterranean, and up rivers and land routes into northern Europe.

The Black Death first started in Central Asia.

ASIA

EUROPE

Flea

Black rat

Black Sea

Mediterranean Sea

AFRICA

THE STORY OF SALT

AS A PRECIOUS AND PORTABLE COMMODITY, SALT HAS LONG BEEN A CENTRAL PART OF HUMAN HISTORY. Humans, like all life, need salt to survive. Some people even believe that the first civilizations began where they did because of the natural deposits of salt found there.

Although it was popular as a food flavoring, it was salt's ability to preserve food that had the biggest impact on the development of the human world. It meant not only that a glut of food grown in summer could be stored and eaten out of season, but also that certain foods could be carried over great distances, meaning longer sea voyages and exploration to foreign lands could take place.

However, salt was difficult to obtain, so it was a highly valued trade item, and even considered as a form of currency by certain peoples. Since its discovery several thousand years ago, salt has become a substance by which fortunes were made and over which wars were fought.

• Humans were processing salt as early as 8,000 years ago, when people living in the area of Shanxi, China, were harvesting salt crystals from salty Lake Yungcheng. Another salt-works in the ancient town of Solnitsata, Bulgaria dates to a couple of thousand years later.
• The main sources of salt are from salt mines, or from the evaporation of seawater (sea salt) and mineral-rich spring water. One of the world's first salt mines was in Hallstatt in modern-day Austria where people began mining for salt in around 800 BCE. The nearby town of Salzburg was a center for salt trading. Its name literally means "city of salt."
• The Egyptians used salt as part of their religious ceremonies, and a

special kind of salt, known as natron (named after the place where it was mined), was used in the preparation of their mummies.
• Salt has been traded since prehistoric times, so much so that "salt routes" were created, along which merchants transported and sold salt in countries where it was not produced. With the spread of civilization, salt became one of the world's main trading commodities.
• Many salt roads, such as the *Via Salaria* in Italy, were established in the Bronze Age. In Britain, the suffix "-wich" in a place-name means it was once a source of salt, as in Sandwich and Norwich.
• Although many ancient civilizations traded in salt—the Greeks, for example, traded salt for

slaves—it was the Romans who exploited its processing and sale through a worldwide network. Roman legionaries were paid in salt or *salarium*, the Latin origin of the word "salary."
• Before the invention of canning or refrigeration, salting was the best-known means of preserving food. During the medieval period, humans used salt to preserve food grown in summer so it could be eaten during the winter months. Meat was also preserved in this way because it was not economic to keep and feed animals through the winter.
• To disguise the salty taste of preserved food, new recipes evolved using spices from the East, such as pepper, cinnamon, cloves, ginger,

cumin, garlic, and mustard.
• In 2200 BCE, the Chinese emperor Hsia Yu levied one of the first known taxes—a tax on salt. Many other leaders all over the world then used this idea as a way to raise revenues. In 1259 the *gabelle*, a salt tax, was introduced in France to pay for the king's conquest of the Kingdom of Naples.
• In Tibet in the 13th century, Marco Polo noted that tiny cakes of salt were pressed with images of the Grand Khan and used as coins. In Africa, salt was used as currency south of the Sahara, and slabs of rock salt were used as coins in Abyssinia.
• 12th-century merchants in Timbuktu, the gateway to the Sahara, valued salt as highly as gold or books.

A BRIEF HIST

IN THE EARLIEST HUMAN SOCIETIES, THERE WAS NO MONEY. To get things, people traded items that had practical value, swapping, say, a fish for an arrowhead, two pots for a fur pelt. This was called bartering, a form of exchanging resources or services that is still used today in certain parts of the world.

Almost all trading before the 6th or 7th centuries BCE was barter trade. However, as human societies became more complex, trading further and further afield with lots of different goods for sale, people needed a standard way of agreeing on the value of things, as well as a way to store their wealth. The need for money was born.

• One of the oldest forms of money was livestock—cows, camels, goats, and other animals—whereby wealth was calculated in terms of the number of animals you owned.
• Early money was nothing like today's coins and banknotes. Instead, it consisted of objects that had a value in themselves, as well as their value as money. Many cultures around the world used different things, including gold, silver, copper, salt, peppercorns, tea, shells, rice, cocoa beans, and barley.
• One of the earliest records of metal being used as money comes from Mesopotamia around 4,500 years ago. There, silver was used as

Clay tokens, c.3500 BCE
These clay tokens were found in city temples in western Asia. They served as counters and perhaps as promises of payment before writing was developed. They came in different sizes and shapes that represented different amounts of the three main traded goods: grain, human labor, and livestock, such as goats and sheep.

Gold, c.1300 BCE
These lumps and rings of gold, silver, and copper give us an insight into Egypt's earliest money system. Measured in units of weight known as deben (around 3oz/90g), these metals could be used to settle bills and to trade in goods.

Manillas, 1500s
Usually made of bronze or copper, manillas originated in the West African kingdom of Calabar. They were made in different weights and shapes, such as the rounded form above, and were often used to buy slaves.

Grzywna, 10th century
This measure of weight, mainly for silver, was commonly used as money in medieval Europe, particularly in the kingdoms of Poland and Bohemia.

Shell money, at least 1600 BCE–200 years ago
Known as the money cowrie, this small species of sea snail was extensively used as shell money in Africa, America, Australia, and Asia. In China, the practice of using cowries began as early as 16th century BCE, and in some countries continued until only 200 years ago. Shells were valued for their beauty but also because they were small and easy to transport, able to withstand

frequent handling and hard to forge. Since they were almost always the same shape and size, they could also be weighed to determine the value of a payment.

In China, real shells were eventually replaced by imitation ones made of copper. Even today, many of the characters in modern Chinese script that relate to money include the ancient symbol for the cowrie shell.

COINS

The first stamped coins produced in the western world came from the kingdom of Lydia (modern-day Turkey) in about 600 BCE. Made of a mixture of gold and silver, their manufacture was strictly controlled to ensure the coins were of a consistent weight and purity. The image stamped on each coin indicated its weight and subsequent value.

The first coins in India were minted of silver c.500 BCE. By the time of the Mauryans, around 200 years later, silver coins were being made in large numbers, cut into an irregular shape of a standard weight and punched with over 450 different symbols, including suns, geometric patterns, wheels, animals, trees, and human figures.

Early Greek coins were mostly made of silver, such as this silver drachma from Aegina, c.400BCE. Later, their gold coins were stamped with the head of the king instead of the lions, bulls, and turtles that had graced the faces of their coins previously.
In 1284, the first ducat gold coins were minted in Venice, center of the gold trade. For the next 500 years, they were the most widely accepted coins since those of the Romans.

Around 200 BCE, the Chinese began to replace knife money with other coins made of metal, some in the shape of spades, then flat discs with a hole in the middle so they could be strung together for easier counting and transport. These copper coins came to be called "cash" and thousands of them could be placed on a single string.

PAPER MONEY

Paper money was first used in China during the Tang dynasty, around 700 CE, having evolved from the trading habit of using receipts for copper as a form of currency instead of the copper itself. In the 13th century, paper money became known in Europe through the accounts of travelers such as Marco Polo but banknotes were not issued in Europe until 1661.

ORY OF MONEY

money because it was highly prized, portable and in regular supply from year to year. Eventually, a shekel (an ancient unit of weight) of silver became the standard currency. One shekel could buy you one month of labor; ten shekels could buy you a slave.

• From these payments made with weighed amounts of silver came the systems of weighed amounts of different metals that have since been used as money in many places around the world. These systems eventually led to the metal coins we know today.

• Carrying around great lumps of silver or piles of peppercorns had obvious drawbacks for growing human civilizations, so the idea of representative money was born, when people started to use— and trust—paper receipts that represented the value of certain goods. These receipts, or notes, worthless in themselves, came to be used as money and eventually currencies as we know them today emerged—systems of money involving metal coins and paper banknotes that are similar all over the world.

Beaver pelts, 17th century
Along with buckskin, beaver pelts were one of the most popular forms of money in the New World, and were often used for trade between European fur traders and Native Americans. The slang term for an American dollar—a "buck"— can be traced back to this time. Fur traders established the beaver pelt as the standard currency: a beaver pelt could buy you 5 pounds of sugar, a pair of shoes or 20 fish hooks!

Rai stones, 1st century
These gigantic limestone discs (over 10ft/3.5m wide) were used as money on the Micronesian island of Yap. The stones were dug up and moved from other islands, and the most valuable ones were those that caused the most deaths during transportation. Because the stones were too large to move, buyers and sellers simply agreed that ownership had changed hands—no physical movement of the stone was required.

Knife money, 1000 BCE
From the 7th century BCE in China small implements made of bronze became a popular form of currency. The implements became smaller over time until they took the form of tokens rather than actual knives. Some even had their values inscribed on them.

Salt bar, 13th century
Salt has always been a precious commodity, worth its weight in gold. In Tibet, according to the explorer Marco Polo, salt was formed into cakes for use as currency, and salt bars were used as money in Ethiopia until the 20th century.

Tea brick, 9th century
Compressed blocks of tea leaves called tea bricks, shown on the left, were also used as currency in parts of Asia.

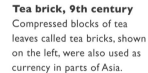

Wampum, 17th century
One of the earliest currencies used in America, wampum consisted of shell beads made by many American Indian tribes. They were adopted by Europeans to trade with the native people of the Americas and became the official currency of New England until 1660. Legend has it that Dutch settlers bought the island of Manhattan from natives using beads. The equivalent price today would be around $1,000.

GOLD

Gold was the first metal widely known to humans. Iron and copper might have allowed us to make more things—helping us to wage war, cook, craft, and thereby develop further as a species—but gold came first. It occurs in a virtually pure state and is the easiest of the metals to work. Its brilliance and permanence (since it neither corrodes nor tarnishes) has led to its association with gods, royalty, immortality and power, and as a symbol of

wealth recognized by many cultures throughout the world.

It is therefore perhaps not surprising that gold, measured out, became money. Its beauty and scarcity gave it value, and the ease by which it could be melted, formed, and measured made it a natural trading medium. Gold (and silver) in standardized coins allowed the economies of the ancient world to expand and prosper. During the Roman Empire, gold and silver flowed to India for spices, and to China for silk. At the height of the

empire (98–160 CE), Roman gold and silver coins could be found from Britain to North Africa and Egypt.

52

Nomads

Traveling the Silk Road could be a dangerous business. Merchants were often attacked by nomads wanting their goods, and raids by Mongol horsemen were the scourge of traders until, in the 13th century under Genghis Khan, the Mongol empire took control of the entire road and made it safe for travel once more.

Horses

Horses were one of the earliest commodities traded along the route. The Han Chinese admired western horses for their larger size, strength, and speed and used them to defeat the nomadic raiders that threatened early traders. Trading in horses led to the beginning of the Silk Road trade network that extended to the Roman empire.

Desert

Some sections of the Silk Road passed through perilous landscapes, such as the Lop Desert. Dunhuang, a city on the desert's eastern edge, became a stopping point for travelers about to start the month-long crossing, where they could load up with water and food.

TRADE ON THE SILK ROAD

IT IS PROBABLE THAT EVEN THE EARLIEST PREHISTORIC TRIBES TRADED GOODS WITH ONE ANOTHER, and by the time of the earliest civilizations, trade routes had spread out to create huge networks that crossed the great land mass of Europe and Asia. People in the ancient world used these networks to buy and sell everything, from natural resources, such as wood, salt, or stone, to wine, food, and goods made by their skilled craftworkers— beautiful objects made from gold, silver and ivory or delicate pots and bowls.

One of the most important and longest-lasting trading routes came to be known as the Silk Road. At its height, it stretched 4,350 miles (7,000 km) from China to Europe. Despite its name, it was not just one road but a large network of routes which had been in use since before the Common Era by traders from China, India, Egypt, Mesopotamia, Rome, and Greece.

Apart from the trading of goods, the great value of the Silk Road lay in the exchange of ideas, beliefs, and cultures among the people traveling along it. Ideas about art, religion, philosophy, science, technology, and every other element of civilization were exchanged, alongside the many things the merchants carried for sale. For centuries, the Silk Road brought different civilizations together, connecting the East with the West.

• Diseases, too, were carried along the road by merchants traveling from city to city. The outbreak of bubonic plague, which decimated the Byzantine Empire in 542 CE, is thought to have arrived there by way of the Silk Road.

• The Silk Road was at its height during China's Tang dynasty and again under the Mongols. But when the Ottomans conquered the Byzantine Empire in the 1450s, they closed the Silk Road and cut all ties with the West. This forced the merchants of the day to take to the sea, beginning the Age of Exploration when new sailing routes led to an even wider trading network.

Cities of the Silk Road

As trade increased along the Silk Road, the stopping places used by merchants turned into towns and eventually into rich and fabulous cities.

• Constantinople, capital of the Byzantine Empire, was one of the main crossing points over the Bosphorus—the strip of water separating Europe from Asia. A rich and powerful city, it was an important meeting point for traders from east and west. When it was captured by the Ottomans, they renamed it Istanbul.

• Chang'an, the ancient capital of China (now named Xi'an), was the starting point for merchants traveling to the west. In the 8th century, it was home to over a million people and was the largest city in the world.

• Kashgar was an ancient oasis town at the edge of the Taklamakan Desert.

The city of Constantinople, an important meeting point for traders

Religion

Religious ideas and beliefs moved along the Silk Road with its travelers and their goods. For example, in the early centuries of the Common Era, the Buddhist religion was introduced into China from India by people traveling the road.

Valuable goods

Merchants of the Silk Road traded many items. From the East came not just silk but porcelain, jade, and lacquerware from China, precious gemstones and spices from India, and silverware from Arabia. From the west came wine, gold, and other goods, such as glass. Many of the trade items were valuable and many of the merchants selling them became hugely rich on the profits of their trade.

Paper, gunpowder, and spices

Some goods sold along the road were more important to the history of the human world than the silk after which it was named. Paper and gunpowder, both invented by the Chinese, helped change the course of history in countries far away from their place of origin. Similarly, the rich spices of the East had a long-lasting impact on the food of myriad civilizations.

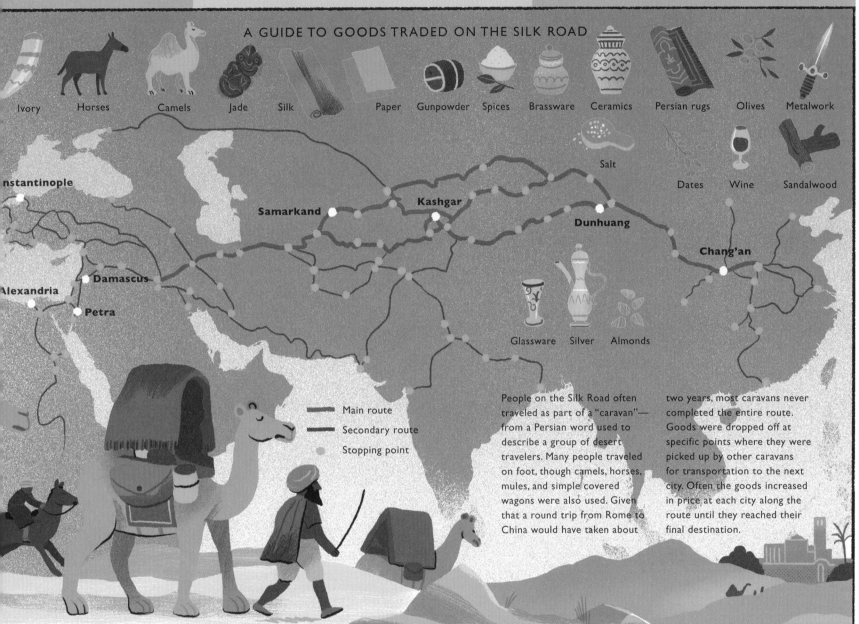

53

A GUIDE TO GOODS TRADED ON THE SILK ROAD

Ivory · Horses · Camels · Jade · Silk · Paper · Gunpowder · Spices · Brassware · Ceramics · Persian rugs · Olives · Metalwork

Salt

Dates · Wine · Sandalwood

Constantinople · Samarkand · Kashgar · Dunhuang · Chang'an · Damascus · Alexandria · Petra

Glassware · Silver · Almonds

— Main route
— Secondary route
● Stopping point

People on the Silk Road often traveled as part of a "caravan"—from a Persian word used to describe a group of desert travelers. Many people traveled on foot, though camels, horses, mules, and simple covered wagons were also used. Given that a round trip from Rome to China would have taken about two years, most caravans never completed the entire route. Goods were dropped off at specific points where they were picked up by other caravans for transportation to the next city. Often the goods increased in price at each city along the route until they reached their final destination.

Silk

The Silk Road gets its name because of the popularity of Chinese silk, which was transported along it to the west, particularly to Rome. In fact, so much gold was shipped out of Rome in exchange for silk during the 1st century that it was eventually banned and various attempts were made to stop Romans wearing fine silk clothing. Despite this, it continued to be one of the most sought-after commodities in Egypt, Greece, Rome, and, later, the Byzantine empire, which started its own silk industry around 500 CE, having stolen the knowledge of silk-making from the Chinese!

Tales of the Orient

In 1271, a young boy named Marco Polo left Italy on a trading trip with his father and uncle that would take them along the Silk Road to the court of the great Mongol warlord Kublai Khan. This great expedition took them over mountains and across great windswept deserts. Arriving at the khan's summer palace of Xanadu in northern China, they quickly became favorites of the Mongol leader and spent nearly 20 years traveling through his empire. On his return, Marco wrote an account of his travels that helped introduce the customs and geography of the East to the Western world.

THE AGE OF

Bartolomeu Dias

In 1487, Portuguese explorer Dias headed south along the west coast of Africa in search of a new route to India. Hit by storms, his ships were blown around the tip of Africa into the Indian Ocean. Even though Dias was forced to turn back, he had proved that Europeans could reach Asia by sea, instead of having to travel overland.

Christopher Columbus

In 1492, Columbus crossed the Atlantic Ocean in search of a new sea route to India from Spain. Sponsored by the Spanish, the expedition sighted land after five weeks, thinking they had reached Asia. They had actually landed in the West Indies, a group of islands close to Central America, and in so doing opened the door to the exploration of a whole new continent, which Europeans called the New World.

Vasco da Gama

Da Gama set sail from Portugal in 1497, tasked with finding a sea route to India. He arrived in India after ten months, by sailing across the Indian Ocean, the first European ever to do so. He went on to visit the Spice Islands and returned to Portugal with many spices that were greeted with great enthusiasm by Europeans. It would be another hundred years before other European powers were able to challenge Portugal's monopoly of this new trading route to the East.

Canada

Newfoundland

NORTH AMERICA

Across the
Pacific Ocean

Atlantic Ocean

Central America

Caribbean

Pacific Ocean

SOUTH AMERICA

This map from 1489 reflects the view of the world at the time. Explorers and traders had reached China, India, and North Africa, but no one had any idea that the Americas existed.

Across
the
Pacific
Ocean

John Cabot

In 1497, an English expedition, led by an Italian captain called John Cabot, set sail across the Atlantic in search of India. He landed instead on Newfoundland off the coast of North America.

Magellan
Straits

TOWARD THE END OF THE MIDDLE AGES, MANY EXPLORERS SET SAIL IN SEARCH OF FAME AND FORTUNE ON THE HIGH SEAS. Thanks to faster and more seaworthy ships and better tools with which they could navigate the world's oceans, they made great discoveries that opened up our understanding of the world.

Much exploration at this time was driven by the demand for exotic goods from India and China—spices, silks, and precious stones like pearls and rubies. Traders from medieval Europe were keen to find new ways to reach the East by sea since the overland routes were long, dangerous, and under the control of various powerful rulers. They were willing to risk great danger to find these new routes—even though many believed that the

southern oceans were boiling hot and filled with monsters!

In 1492, a man named Christopher Columbus took such a risk. Most people at this time still thought that the world was flat, but Columbus thought that it was round and that by sailing west from Europe you could reach China. Little did he know that there was a whole new continent unknown to the West— the Americas—laying in between.

Encouraged by their western rulers, particularly the Spanish, Dutch, French, English, and Portuguese, the explorers of the time would make many further discoveries that would eventually lead to the colonization of America and, as European countries vied with each other for possession of newly discovered lands, to the destruction of the great civilizations that they found there.

EXPLORATION

54

Francis Drake

The English explorer and privateer Francis Drake was the first captain to sail all around the world. His expedition took nearly three years, from 1577 to 1580, and only one of his five ships, the *Golden Hind*, made it home. During his many expeditions, he captured Spanish ships for their treasure and looted some of the Spanish colonies in the Caribbean. On his return, Drake was knighted by Queen Elizabeth I for his privateering services to the English crown.

EUROPE

China

India

Jacques Cartier

In 1534, French explorer Jacques Cartier explored the east coast of modern-day Canada in a search for a new sailing route to China. Using native North Americans as his guides, he eventually canoed up the St. Lawrence river to reach a small village that he named Montreal.

AFRICA

Spice Islands

Indian Ocean

AUSTRALIA

Arctic Ocean

Amerigo Vespucci

Seven years after Columbus's first voyage, another Italian reached the mainland of America, sailing down the coast of South America as far as the mouth of the Amazon River in northern Brazil. The continent was named after him in 1507.

Ferdinand Magellan

In 1519, five ships commanded by Ferdinand Magellan left Spain, tasked with finding a sea route to Asia across the Atlantic. He discovered just such a route, sailing through a narrow channel at the tip of South America, now known as the Magellan Straits, which linked the Atlantic and Pacific Oceans. Three years later, one of the ships, the *Vittoria*, finally made it back home. Magellan died during the expedition, but the *Vittoria* was the very first ship to have sailed all around the world.

IN SEARCH OF GOLD

Gold Inca figure

Columbus's discovery of the New World, and the tales of the riches with which he returned, brought a wave of ambitious Spaniards, known as the Conquistadors, in his wake. Seeking fame and fortune, hundreds of them sailed to the Americas in the early 1500s in a quest for gold, but not all succeeded.
• In 1519, Hernán Cortés mounted an expedition, landing in what is now present-day Mexico. He amassed a vast army of native people who wanted to rebel against the Aztec rulers and marched on the Aztec capital of Tenochtitlan. Eventually, after fighting both Aztecs and rival Conquistadors, he conquered the Aztec empire.
• Drawn by reports of Peru's riches, Francisco Pizarro led two failed expeditions before finally succeeding in conquering the Inca empire in 1532. He arrived with just 180 men but managed to kidnap the Inca leader Atahualpa and demanded a huge ransom for his return before killing him anyway. Apart from such brutal treatment at the hands of their European conquerors, many of the Native Americans were wiped out by diseases brought from the West against which they had no protection.

Gold Aztec pendant

WE ARE WHAT WE EAT

TODAY, THE FOOD WE EAT OFTEN USES INGREDIENTS GROWN ON THE OTHER SIDE OF THE WORLD, cooked according to recipes from countries that we've never even visited. However, this is a recent development. For most of human history, we have had to rely on the food that we could hunt or gather from our local environment in order to stay alive.

The first thing that changed what we humans ate on a daily basis was the advent of farming—where we took wild plants and animals and cultivated or tamed them over many years to give us better-quality food, a process known as domestication. It gave us bigger grains, better yields of milk and meat, and a regular supply of new foods, like flour for bread. But our diets were still made up largely of local produce and the distinctive cuisine (cooking style) of our homeland.

As civilizations grew and spread, so too did the trade of goods between them. Trading in food—the selling of plants or animals from one place to another—started thousands of years ago, with ingredients traded from continent to continent, transported across oceans and deserts, widening not just the foods we ate but those that we adopted to grow or raise ourselves. Not all foods were readily accepted by new cultures, however. It took 300 years for tomatoes to become widely accepted in Europe. 16th-century doctors believed that they were poisonous and the cause of "melancholic humors"!

FOOD PRESERVATION

Finding ways to preserve food was of great importance to early humans. It meant they no longer had to eat everything they had grown or killed immediately but could keep some for later use. Having a stable food supply for the future meant that people no longer had to try to find food every day, and this, along with farming, let humans live in one place and form communities.

Many cultures preserved their food using the same basic methods. Accidental fermentation of grape juice or the curdling of milk led to wine- and cheese-making. Meat or fish left to hang in the smoke from a fire showed people you could preserve meat through smoking, and the creation of butter may have come as a result of nomadic people carrying their milk with them in wooden barrels.

• Middle Eastern and oriental cultures were drying foods to preserve them as early as 12000 BCE. By the Middle Ages, purpose-built "still houses" with a small oven in them were created to dry fruits, vegetables, and herbs in areas that did not have enough strong sunlight for drying to take place naturally.

• Many early cultures also used salt to help remove the moisture from foods. Salting was common and even became a culinary art, by choosing different types of salt to flavor the salted goods (rock salt, sea salt, spiced salt, and so on.).
• Pickling (preserving foods in vinegar or another acid) is also an ancient form of food preservation. The Romans pickled all sorts of fish, meats, and vegetables.
• Making jams or jellies to preserve fruit through the use of honey or sugar was a technique known to the earliest cultures, including the ancient Greeks.

COLUMBIAN EXCHANGE

One great cultural exchange in food occurred when Europeans began to explore the New World (the Americas) for the first time in the 1500s. They traded in many different foods, plants, and types of livestock in an event known as the Columbian Exchange, which introduced many new foods to countries around the world. Most trading in livestock involved new animals being introduced into the New World from the Old. One of the first European exports to the Americas, the horse, had a fundamental effect on many Native American tribes, giving them a whole new means of transport. Many tribes expanded their territories thanks to horses, which were considered so valuable that horse herds became a measure of wealth. Unfortunately, it was not just food that was introduced from one culture to another. Many diseases were also accidentally transferred and huge numbers of Native Americans died as result.

NEW WORLD
Fruit and vegetables: Avocados, beans, chili peppers, cocoa, peanuts, pineapples, potatoes, sweet potatoes, squashes, tomatoes.
Spices: Allspice, paprika, vanilla
Grains: Corn (maize)
Livestock: Turkeys
Diseases: Syphilis

OLD WORLD
Fruit and vegetables: Bananas, oranges, lemons, coffee, olives, onions, peaches, pears, sugar cane.
Grains: Barley, oats, rice, wheat.
Livestock: Chickens, cows, donkeys, horses, mules, pigs, sheep.
Diseases: Chickenpox, influenza, smallpox, malaria, measles, yellow fever.

THE GREAT FOOD EXCHANGE

When cultures meet, it's not just their religion, language, or clothing that may be different. Often the food they eat and the recipes they use will be vastly different too. People on both sides often discover a huge range of previously unknown foods—and new opportunities for trading in them! This map shows the origin of some common food plants and their spread around the world.

First grown by the Aztecs in Mexico, there are records of **tomatoes** being used in cooking by 500 CE. Like the potato, tomatoes were first brought back to Europe from the Americas by the Spanish and soon spread to their colonies abroad.

Potatoes were traded in South America as a valuable source of food as early as 5000 BCE. The Conquistadors took them to Spain from Peru in the 1500s, and their use spread across Europe, though Sir Walter Raleigh claimed to have introduced the potato to England separately in 1586.

Cocoa was being used to make a cold, spicy drink in Central America over 3,000 years ago. The Spanish brought it back with them in the 1520s and added sugar to make the sweet, hot drink we know today.

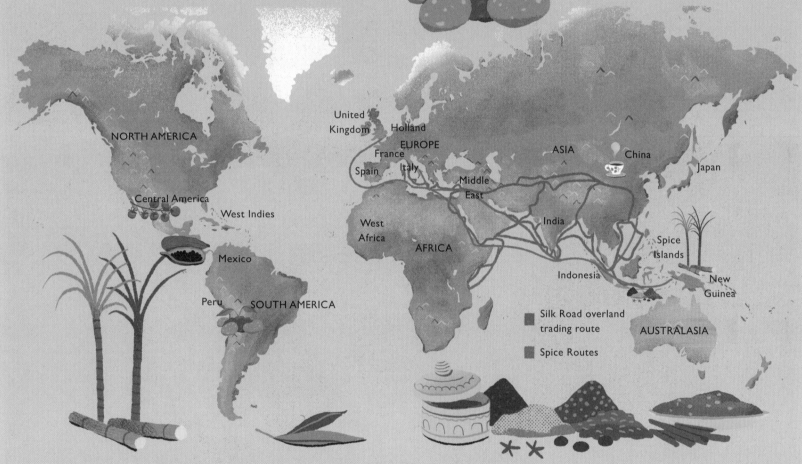

NORTH AMERICA

United Kingdom

Holland

EUROPE

France

Spain

Italy

ASIA

China

Japan

Central America

West Indies

Middle East

West Africa

AFRICA

India

Spice Islands

Mexico

Indonesia

New Guinea

Peru

SOUTH AMERICA

■ Silk Road overland trading route

■ Spice Routes

AUSTRALASIA

First grown on the island of New Guinea, **sugar cane** was first used to produce a sweet juice over 8,000 years ago. Its use soon spread throughout Southeast Asia and then to the wider world. Granulated sugar was first produced in the 1st century and by 1500 sugar was a valuable commodity—a 100lb bag (45kg) was worth as much as an ounce (28g) of gold. By the mid-1500s, sugar cane was grown in Spanish colonies throughout the West Indies and became one of the main exports from Latin America.

Tea drinking was established in China centuries before it had ever been heard of in the West, but by the early 1600s, Dutch traders had established a trading post on the island of Java, in Indonesia, and used it to ship tea from China to Holland. Tea drinking soon became fashionable in Europe, but because of its high price, it remained a drink for the wealthy.

The trade in **spices** developed throughout Asia and the Middle East as long ago as 2000 BCE. The word "spice" comes from the Latin *species,* which means an item of special value, and in the ancient world, spices had ritual and medicinal value as well as their use as food flavorings. Many spices only grew in the tropical East, especially in the Moluccas, known as the Spice Islands—the origin of fragrant spices such as cloves and nutmeg.

During the Middle Ages spices were among the most highly demanded and expensive products

available in Europe—the most common being black pepper, cinnamon, cumin, nutmeg, ginger, and cloves. New dishes with exotic flavors and colors found their way onto the medieval table. Though expensive, spices were seen as a sign of status and also helped disguise the salty taste of preserved meat and fish.

From the 8th until the 15th century, Venice was the center for the European spice trade and became rich as a result. By the end of the Middle Ages, it's estimated about 1,000 tons of pepper were imported into western Europe each year.

CONQUERING THE OCEANS

North Pole

Lines of longitude

Equator

Lines of latitude

South Pole

THE AGE OF EXPLORATION, from the 1400 to 1600s, marked a time when many European nations set forth to explore the world. These oceanic explorers needed better means of finding their way and, although humans had been using their knowledge of the heavens as a guide to navigation since ancient times, this period saw a great leap forward in the application of mathematics and astronomy to the problem, leading to the invention of many new navigational tools. These new tools allowed explorers to find their position at sea, pinpoint the location of their discoveries in order to return to them, and thereby establish trade routes between these newfound lands and home.

• The intrepid explorers of the ancient world may not have had these tools, but they had their own amazing methods of navigating the world's oceans—watching the direction of the waves and the flight of birds and observing the movement of stars and clouds. The Polynesians colonized the most far-flung islands of the

Pacific using these methods, recording the information on maps made of sticks.

• The sailors of medieval ships sailed using knowledge acquired over many years, often using pre-established routes where it was unusual to go more than a day or two out of sight of the coast.

• Ocean navigation in the Age of Exploration, however, necessitated long periods without land in sight. This drove the need for compasses and nautical charts and reinforced the importance of using the stars to determine one's position. Certain instruments used by Muslim astronomers for centuries, such as the astrolabe and quadrant, were adapted and simplified for use at sea.

• Navigators used the imaginary lines of latitude and longitude to help determine their position and chart their routes. Crisscrossing the globe, lines of latitude run parallel to the Equator, dividing the globe from north to south; lines of longitude run from pole to pole, dividing the globe from east to west.

Cross-staff

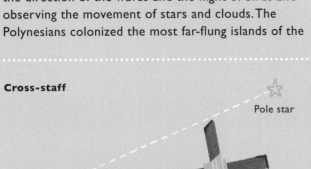

Pole star

Eye

Horizon

The **astrolabe** and **cross-staff** were both used to determine latitude by measuring the angle between the horizon and Polaris, also called the North or Pole Star, or another heavenly body.

Astrolabe

Pole Star

Horizon

Polynesian stick map

The **magnetic compass** had been developed in China in the 2nd century CE but its use did not spread to Europe for hundreds of years. By the 16th century, it had become an indispensable tool for ocean going navigators allowing them to determine their direction, day or night, fair weather or foul.

Before the invention of clocks, navigators used a **sandglass** to keep track of time. Sandglasses were used in combination with a **log**, a piece of wood attached to a line, knotted at uniform intervals. This would be thrown overboard, and a sailor would count the number of knots that passed through his fingers against a turn of the one-minute glass to work out the speed of the ship in nautical miles per hour ("knots").

A **traverse board** was used to record the course of a ship. It consisted of a circular piece of wood marked with the compass points, and a system of pegs and holes around its edge, attached to the center by pieces of string. The pegs were moved every half hour to reflect the direction in which the ship was heading.

DISCOVERY AND INVENTION

TOWARD THE END OF THE MEDIEVAL PERIOD, HUMANS STARTED TO ASK MORE QUESTIONS ABOUT THE WORLD AROUND THEM. In Europe, people rediscovered the writings of ancient Greece and Rome, and their ideas about mathematics, art, and philosophy. Fired by these discoveries and influenced by the exchange of ideas from other newly discovered parts of the world, they began to try out new theories based on what they had learned. This movement, known as the Renaissance (meaning "rebirth"), lasted from the 14th to the 17th centuries and marked one of the most important periods in human development.

As well as an explosion in the arts, this period also saw the birth of many new inventions and scientific discoveries, from the mechanical clock and the printing press to the navigational tools that helped Columbus to discover the New World. Toward the end of the Renaissance, this study of the world and how it worked ushered in an age of scientific revolution. From Copernicus's realization that the Earth revolved around the sun to Isaac Newton's theory of gravity, the great thinkers of the day made discoveries that would change our understanding of many things, paving the way for the modern era.

New ways of seeing

This period saw great improvements in the making of lenses, which in turn led to the invention of the first telescopes and microscopes. The earliest-known working telescope appeared in the Netherlands in 1608, though its design was greatly improved by Galileo the following year. Isaac Newton is credited with constructing the first reflecting telescope in 1668, which used a series of mirrors to create a better-quality image. The earliest known example of a microscope also appeared in Europe in the early 1600s and was developed further by Galileo who built his version in 1625.

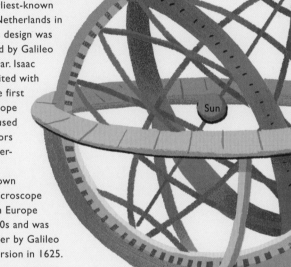

Copernican celestial sphere

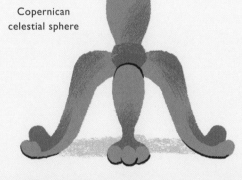

Newton's reflecting telescope

Galileo's microscope

Instruments for measuring

Many new scientific instruments were invented during this time, supporting a novel way of thinking about science that was based on experiment and observation.

• In the late 1500s, Galileo designed a thermoscope, a precursor to the modern thermometer, which could detect changes in temperature.

• Inspired by Galileo, Italian physicist Evangelista Torricelli is credited with inventing the first working barometer in 1643, using a tube of mercury to measure atmospheric pressure.

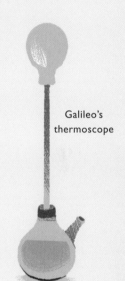

Galileo's thermoscope

Understanding the universe

The armillary or celestial sphere, a scientific instrument representing the movement of the planets, had existed since the time of the ancient Greeks, but then it was shown with the Earth at its center. In 1543, Polish astronomer Nicolas Copernicus described the true nature of the solar system. The new Copernican armillary spheres, with the sun at their center, were among the first complex mechanical devices ever made. Many portraits of the period feature famous figures resting one hand on an armillary sphere to represent the height of wisdom and knowledge.

Early barometer

A VISION OF THE FUTURE

Leonardo da Vinci was one of the great geniuses of the Renaissance. He was an artist, architect, musician, and scientist, and his sketchbooks held drawings of many different inventions, from parachutes to submarines, robotic knights, and armored vehicles. While many of his ideas never progressed beyond his sketches, they inspired generations of inventors that followed, and provided a glimpse of the world of amazing machines that fill our world today.

Sundial, c.4000 BCE
Shadow cast by the sun moves around the dial as the day progresses

Water clock, c.1400 BCE

Clock candle, 11th century
Notches record hours

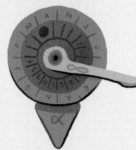

Star dial, 16th century
Time read off outer dial once center hole is aligned with Polaris

Chinese fire clock, c.1100
Incense stick holder. Weights suspended by silk threads.

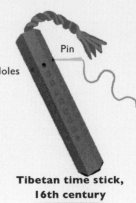

Holes — Pin

Tibetan time stick, 16th century

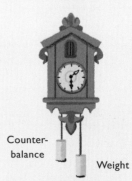

Sand clock, 8th century

Counter-balance — Weight

Mechanical clock, 17th century

Pendulum

Pendulum clock, 1657

Pocket watch, 1524

A QUESTION OF TIME

HUMANS HAVE ALWAYS WANTED TO KNOW THE TIME, WHETHER TO HELP WITH FARMING, KNOW WHEN NIGHT WILL FALL, OR—MUCH LATER—TURN UP TO WORK ON TIME. Ancient humans told the time by watching the shadows cast by the sun as it moved across the sky; at night, they used the movement of the stars. Later, humans invented all manner of timekeeping devices, until the invention of the mechanical clock overtook everything that had come before it.

• Our current system of time measurement uses a number system with 60 as its base (for example, there are 60 minutes in an hour). It originated with the ancient Sumerians some 5,000 years ago.

• The Egyptians, as well as using large obelisks to track the movement of the sun, also developed water clocks, which measured time by the flow of water through a vessel with a small hole in it.

• Many timekeeping devices have either tracked the sun or stars, like the sun or star dial, or measured a certain period of time, like the clock candle, the sand clock, and the Chinese fire clock. In the latter, lighted incense sticks released weights as the stick gradually burned through the threads that held them.

• Tibetan time sticks worked rather like sundials, using the shadow cast by a pin inserted through a wooden stick.

• Early mechanical clocks were invented in Europe and used in many monasteries and cathedrals during the 14th century. In fact, before most households had clocks, human communities often kept track of time by listening out for their local church bells.

• These early clocks, powered by falling weights, were the standard timekeeping device until the pendulum clock was invented in 1656. This clock used a weight that swung backward and forward to keep time.

• In the 16th century, clockmakers began to use a coiled spring, which, once wound, released its energy to drive the clock. This made smaller clocks possible, and in 1524 the pocket watch was invented in Germany.

A WORLD IN PRINT

THE INVENTION OF THE PRINTING PRESS by Johannes Gutenberg around the year 1450 was one of the greatest events in the history of human communication. Together with his invention of moveable metal type, it meant that books could be produced quickly and in quantity, leading to an information revolution perhaps only matched by the arrival of the internet over 500 years later.

At the time, the human world was experiencing great change. As the medieval period drew to a close, an era of enlightenment emerged, full of new ideas and discoveries. Thanks to Gutenberg's inventions, this new thinking could be made more widely known, with people able to read books and leaflets that were printed cheaply, quickly, and in quantity. This did a great deal to help the study of science and many other branches of knowledge and eventually led to an increase in literacy.

• Hand printing—using blocks to print patterns or words by hand onto material or paper—had been known for hundreds of years. But Gutenberg's invention combined a mechanical press with blocks of mass-produced moveable metal type, which made the whole process much quicker and easier to manage.

• The type was arranged to make blocks of text that were then rolled over with ink, covered with paper, and then moved under the press. This pushed the paper against the inky blocks to make pages of type that could be bound into books. This could be repeated to make many copies of a book in a world where books were still mainly handwritten and therefore in scarce supply.

• Gutenberg's first book was a Bible printed in Latin, but he also made a book of grammar, a dictionary, a psalter (or psalm book), and several other volumes.

• Gutenberg's invention spread rapidly. By the end of the 15th century, there were more than 1,000 printers in Europe, the most important in England being William Caxton, who printed the first books in English. One of the first large books he printed was Geoffrey Chaucer's *Canterbury Tales*.

The **Gutenberg Bible** was the first major book printed using mass-produced moveable metal type in Europe. It marked the start of the "Gutenberg Revolution" and the age of the printed book in the West.

A piece of moveable metal type

A 15th-century printer checking a page of type

A BRIEF HISTORY OF BOOKS

FOR THOUSANDS OF YEARS, BOOKS HAVE PROVIDED A VITAL RECORD OF HUMAN LIFE—our achievements, and our growing body of knowledge about all things. Since we first invented writing, we have used books to store our thoughts and beliefs, as well as the experiences of both individuals and whole societies, preserving them to be read by others long after the death of the author.

Books provide us with a window into our human past. Many ideas and thoughts that have occurred to humans through the ages can be found in them, from religious teachings and the wisdom of great thinkers to the stories, poetry, and plays of great writers—as alive and fresh for us today as they were when they were first written.

• The Romans were the first people to make books that look like those we know today, but all their books were written by hand on parchment (a kind of paper made from the skin of animals). For hundreds of years, every book in the world had to be handwritten and it was not until the invention of the printing press in the middle of the 15th century that more than one copy of a book could be made at a time.

• In medieval times, reading was an important activity in the lives of monks, who were often the only people in a town or village who could read and write. Most monasteries had a scriptorium—a workroom where monks worked to create illuminated manuscripts, copying and decorating important works so they could be preserved and shared.

FROM CLAY TO PAPER—A TIMELINE OF BOOK DEVELOPMENT

The first books were not made of paper. **Over 5,000 years ago,** the Sumerians kept extensive records of everything, carved in a form of writing called cuneiform onto clay tablets. The name "cuneiform" means "wedge-shaped."

Then came the Egyptians, **4,000 years ago,** with their papyrus scrolls, long strips of paper-like material, some many yards long, that recorded in hieroglyphs everything from medicinal cures to records of taxes. The scrolls were wrapped around a stick when not in use.

By **1300 BCE,** the Chinese were making books from strips of bamboo, which had holes put in them and were then tied together with silken cord. These bundles are where the Chinese word meaning "volume" comes from.

By **500 BCE** parchment (a thin material made from the untanned skins of animals, particularly sheep, calves and goats) had been developed as a cheaper substitute for papyrus and was used extensively by the Greeks and Romans.

By **200 BCE** the Greeks and Romans were using blocks of wood coated in wax that, once set, could be written on using a stylus. These wax tablets were sometimes joined together with cords, like an early form of ring binder!

By **300 CE,** scrolls began to be replaced by the codex, a book made of a number of sheets attached at one edge. The format was considered more effective and convenient, and it is still the standard book form over 1,500 years later.

Folded codices— where a continuous scroll is folded into a concertina for easy reading—were also known. The Mayans created them from **c.500 CE** from lengths of bark cloth or animal hide, using them to record the history of their gods.

LIBRARIES

• At Nineveh, once the largest city in the world, the ancient kings of Assyria created one of the world's first libraries. It contained over 20,000 clay tablets. Dating from the 7th century BCE, they were inscribed with texts of all kinds, including the Epic of Gilgamesh.

• The Library of Alexandria in Egypt was one of the largest and most important libraries of the ancient world. Created by the ancient Greeks, it contained as many as 400,000 papyrus scrolls. It was partially destroyed by fire in 47BCE and much of its contents destroyed.

• To protect books from theft, chained libraries were created where the books were attached to their shelves by a chain. This was long enough for the books to be taken out and read, but not for them to be removed from the library. The practice was common from the Middle Ages to the 18th century.

A WORLD OF STORIES

Very few early books were concerned with the telling of stories, often being filled instead with accounts of battles, taxes paid, or sacred writings of one sort or another. For entertainment, people listened to stories instead, told by minstrels or passed down by word of mouth from their elders—stories of heroes and gods, of battles and the lives of kings and queens, or tales of giants, fairies, and strange mythical beasts. Such tales were told over and over, long before they were printed into books or even written down. It is only in the last few hundred years that the majority of humans in the world have learned to read and had books so readily available that they have become central to our way of life.

THE OLDEST TALE

History's oldest-known fictional story is probably the *Epic of Gilgamesh*, a mythic poem written on 12 clay tablets sometime between 1500 and 1200 BCE and discovered in the ruins of the great library at Nineveh. The tale centers on a Sumerian king named Gilgamesh who goes on a classic hero's journey that sees him slay monsters, meet the gods, and search for the key to immortality. The tale can still be read today, available in hardback, paperback, and as an e-book edition. There is only one original copy available, and that is at the British Museum!

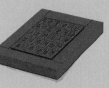

Around **500 CE,** illustrations began to be added to handwritten manuscripts (known as illuminated manuscripts), often decorated with intricate designs in striking colors and embellished with silver or gold.

In **868 CE,** the first book printed using woodblock printing was made in China. The blocks were carved with raised Chinese characters in reverse, which were then covered in ink and pressed onto the surface of a scroll to create a print.

Around **150 CE,** paper as we know it was invented in China, made by pulping flax fibers before flattening and drying them in the sun. Paper gradually replaced parchment, but it was not used widely in Europe until the 14th century.

In the **1st and 2nd centuries,** various forms of moveable type were created—individual characters that could be moved around and reused to print documents. The first book printed using moveable metal type was made in Korea, *c.*1377.

By **1450,** the first moveable type in Europe was developed by Johannes Gutenberg. Regarded as one of the most important inventions of the human world, it revolutionized the spread of information by making books available to the masses.

By the end of the **15th century,** printing had spread to no fewer than 236 countries with more than 20 million books produced. From this point onward, the printed book was in universal use throughout Europe, although most were still printed in Latin.

CHANGING TIMES

BY THE END OF THE 1500S, HUMAN UNDERSTANDING OF THE WORLD AND OUR PLACE IN IT WAS BEGINNING TO CHANGE. The discoveries of explorers made people realize that the world was much bigger than previously thought, while at the same time scientists were revealing that the Earth was only a small part of a much greater universe—and not at the center of it either. In Europe, people had begun to emerge from the narrow confines of life in the Middle Ages and to change the way they thought about how life should be lived, that it should not be just about hard work and wars and the strict teachings of the Church. European society had changed too. The Black Death had killed millions of people and helped to change the structure of society for those that survived, helping to bring an end to the feudal system and allowing a new class of citizens to emerge, rich from the new trade opportunities and keen to display their wealth.

During this period, there was a remarkable flowering of art, culture, and science, starting in Italy and spreading to encompass most of Western Europe. Inspired by the rediscovery of important works from ancient Greece and Rome, Italian scholars, artists, and thinkers abandoned the pessimism of medieval times, revived an interest in learning and a renewed belief that people, rather than God, could control their own lives and be capable of great things. This movement, which later became known as the Renaissance (meaning "rebirth"), lasted from the late 14th to the early 17th centuries. It marked an important period in human development and an expansion in human knowledge that would mark the start of the modern world.

EDUCATION

In medieval Europe, the Church was the main center of education and few people other than priests or other religious officials could read or write. During the Renaissance, this began to change and, among the wealthy, being educated became seen as important and desirable. The children of the wealthy were taught the writings of the Greeks and Romans and encouraged to become accomplished at music, art, and foreign languages. The ideal was to become a "Universal man or woman," skillful and educated in a wide range of subjects, from science and philosophy to literature and the arts. Many new universities opened throughout Europe during this time and the development of the printing press and the availability of books helped to spread new ideas far and wide. This, together with the foundation of public libraries, helped to create a more literate population who would form the basis of the modern world.

HUMANISM

Renaissance thinkers believed that the mortal world, including the many achievements of which humans were capable, was the most significant part of God's creation. They believed that rather than dwelling on the afterlife (as had been the major preoccupation in Medieval times), humans should be inspired to achieve great things in their earthly life and—with education, faith in God, and a new spirit of optimism for the future—they could create a better society for all. From this developed humanism, a philosophy that placed great value on human dignity, moral values, and the importance of learning. Humanists believed that people could shape their own destiny and through education could learn to better serve their society for the common good, using experiment and experience as the basis of their knowledge, rather than following the traditions or superstitions of the past.

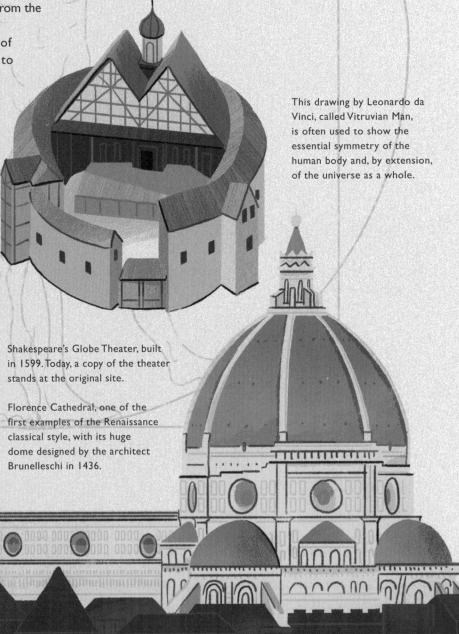

This drawing by Leonardo da Vinci, called Vitruvian Man, is often used to show the essential symmetry of the human body and, by extension, of the universe as a whole.

Shakespeare's Globe Theater, built in 1599. Today, a copy of the theater stands at the original site.

Florence Cathedral, one of the first examples of the Renaissance classical style, with its huge dome designed by the architect Brunelleschi in 1436.

THE REFORMATION

In 16th-century Europe the Roman Catholic Church was all powerful. Many of its officials had become rich and corrupt and this, along with the new spirit of enquiry, led some people to question the Church's authority and ask for change. In 1517, a German priest named Martin Luther, shown here, demanded reform, including a return to simple ceremonies, use of the local languages rather than Latin, and an uncorrupted clergy. Luther's ideas soon gained support and this movement—known as the Reformation—eventually created a split between traditional Christians (Catholics) and the supporters of Luther, known as Protestants.

PATRONS

During the Renaissance many wealthy people supported artists, paying them and encouraging them to create new works. Known as patrons, they included rich merchants, princes, popes, and noble families. Among the most powerful patrons of the Renaissance were the Medicis, a family of bankers from Florence, Italy, who helped to make their city an artistic and cultural center during the period. Lorenzo de' Medici, shown here, was one of the most powerful and enthusiastic patrons, sponsoring artists such as Michelangelo and Botticelli.

ART AND ARTISTS

During much of the medieval period, European artists had painted mainly religious subjects but with the Renaissance came a new way of painting that would change the course of human art. Not only did artists begin to paint portraits, landscapes, and scenes from legends as well as religious scenes, but they created daring new works that used realism to great effect, painting things to look as lifelike as possible. They used real models for their work and developed the technique of perspective to give a sense of depth and space to their paintings and drawings, quite unlike the two-dimensional works of the medieval period. They studied anatomy and examined dead bodies to help them understand how bones and muscles worked, thereby advancing our understanding of the human body. Some of the greatest works of art in the world were created during this time, from Leonardo da Vinci's *Mona Lisa* and Sandro Botticelli's *Birth of Venus*, to Michelangelo's *David*, regarded as one of the most perfect sculptures of the human figure ever made.

Vanishing point

Artists in the Renaissance used perspective and the idea of a "vanishing point" to show distant objects getting increasingly smaller until they are too far away to see.

Painting and sculpture were not the only arts to be revolutionized. Theater was transformed, not least by the arrival of the period's most famous playwright William Shakespeare. New plays were written, built around stories of romance, tragedy, and adventure rather than the religious plays that had gone before.

Renaissance architects, too, aspired to create new buildings as grand and elegant as those of ancient Greece and Rome, studying mathematics and geometry to help them design buildings with many pillars, arches, and domes in the classical style.

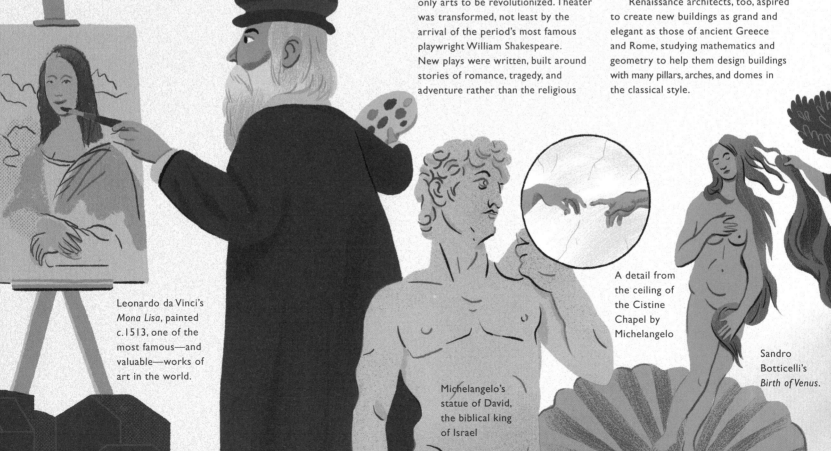

Leonardo da Vinci's *Mona Lisa*, painted c.1513, one of the most famous—and valuable—works of art in the world.

Michelangelo's statue of David, the biblical king of Israel

A detail from the ceiling of the Cistine Chapel by Michelangelo

Sandro Botticelli's *Birth of Venus*.

THE MODERN WORLD

IT IS A CURIOUS THOUGHT THAT, BIOLOGICALLY SPEAKING, TODAY'S HUMANS ARE THE SAME AS OUR ANCESTORS WHO WANDERED THE AFRICAN PLAINS 200,000 YEARS AGO, BUT THE WORLD IN WHICH THEY LIVE COULD NOT BE MORE DIFFERENT. In the last 500 years, the rate at which the world has changed has been enormous. Encompassing the Industrial Revolution of the 18th century and the Digital Revolution of recent times, our ability to invent new technology to help us master the world around us has escalated exponentially. It took nearly 500 years for Leonardo da Vinci's dreams of a flying machine to become reality, yet only a single generation between the flight of the Wright brothers and Neil Armstrong's "one small step" on the moon. It is this cultural evolution that has helped make us humans such a force in the history of life on Earth. Rather than adapting through natural selection like all the other creatures with which we share our planet, we have the means and the intelligence to change our environment to meet our needs, inventing machines to do our work for us. It is hard to imagine that just a few generations ago there was no electricity, no telephones, no computers, no cars or airplanes, no antibiotics or heart transplants, no World Wide Web or satellites traveling to the far reaches of space. And our human story is by no means over yet. Who knows what the human world will look like in another 500 years, or even in a hundred? What is certain is that it will be as different from the world today as our modern existence is from that of medieval humans, or as theirs was from their ancient ancestors. But at the same time we will likely still be surrounded by reminders of our past—the great buildings or precious objects that survive to tell us their own story of human history.

Index

Glossary of terms

Agriculture—farming land and keeping animals for food, wool, and other products

Amulet—a small item or piece of jewelry that was thought to keep away disease, danger, and evil

Artifact—something made by a human being, which tells us about the time and place it was created

Astronomy—the study of the sun, moon, stars, and planets

Black Death—a fast-moving outbreak of the bubonic plague across Europe and Asia in the 14th century

Bronze Age—the period of time when weapons and tools began to be made of bronze rather than stone

Cargo—goods carried from one place to another for trade

Civilization—the society, culture, and way of life of an area

Community—a group of people that live together

Cuisine—the type of food and way it is cooked in an area

Culture—the ideas and practices of a group of people

Democracy—a society in which everyone is equal, usually by having a say in who their rulers are

Development—a new and advanced idea or way of doing something

Domestication—taming an animal and keeping it either as a pet or on a farm

Emperor—the ruler of an empire

Empire—a large group of countries or states that are ruled over by a single leader or group

Evolution—how living things have changed from earlier forms during the history of the Earth

Feudalism—a society in which royal or noble families allow people to live on their land in return for a share of their crops and their help during wartime

Gladiator—a man trained to fight other men and animals in arenas during Roman times

Hominin—an early human-like creature

Homo sapiens—the scientific name for human beings

Humanism—the idea that humans should not look to religion for help in living their life but trust in their own ability

Humor—one of the four fluids that were thought to make up the human body in medieval times (blood, phlegm, yellow bile, and black bile, the "four humors"), which were thought to determine a person's appearance and nature

Hunter-gatherer—early human who moved from place to place, hunting, fishing, and collecting wild food

Ice Age—a cold period in the history of the Earth when more of the planet's surface was covered in ice than today

Iron Age—the period that followed the Bronze Age, when weapons and tools began to be made of iron rather than bronze

Manuscript—a book or document that has been written by hand, not printed

Megalith—a large stone that either alone or with others forms a monument from prehistoric times

Merchant—someone who trades in goods or services

Mourning—a time when you feel sad after someone has died

Neanderthal—an early human that lived in Ice Age Europe between 120,000 and 35,000 years ago

Network—a group of people that are linked in some way

Philosophy—the study of life, truth, and knowledge

Prehistoric—from the time before written records

Preserve—to treat food in some way so that it doesn't go bad, such as by salting or smoking

Reformation—a 16th-century movement that aimed to bring about changes to the Roman Church and that ended in creating new religions, such as Protestantism

Renaissance—a way of describing the great interest in ancient times during the Middle Ages, which led to many developments in art and literature

Resources—the materials available to a group of people

Revolution—an important and wide-ranging change

Siege—in war, when enemy troops surround a town or castle and cut off the people inside from essential supplies in the hope that they will surrender

Silk Road—an ancient series of roads that linked China with the eastern Mediterranean, which were used for carrying goods, such as silk and spices, between the two areas and farther afield

Slavery—buying and selling people against their will to become slaves, mostly to do hard and unpleasant work

Solstice—the summer solstice is when the sun is at its highest point in the year (longest day) and the winter solstice is when the sun is at its lowest point in the year (shortest day)

Spice—a strong-smelling substance that comes from plants that is mostly used to flavor food and drinks

Stone Age—the period that came before the Bronze Age, when weapons and tools were made of stone and other natural materials, such as bone, wood, and horn

Tax—a payment to a ruler that is required by law

Temple—a building for worshipping gods

Theater—a place where plays and other performances are given

Trade—the exchange of money for goods and services

Treason—when someone is not loyal to their country or ruler